I0063598

Propelling Performance

WHY YOUR BUSINESS IS STALLING AND WHAT YOU CAN DO ABOUT IT

ROBERT NANKERVIS

Rob's quarterly planning sessions have help changed the direction and focus of the Cutri Fruit business for the better, having tried many times to self-implement without success. Working with Rob allowed us to dissect what made our business thrive so that we could then focus on what was important. This has been the single most important change for our business, bringing absolute clarity on where we are heading and what needs to be achieved to get there – every session with Rob has felt like we nailed it. Thank you.

Gaethan Cutri – Owner, Cutri Fruit

Rob has been great at helping and focusing our Management Team on strategic planning and establishing more rigorous goal setting processes through our quarterly workshops. His personality and skill sets have really made this an enjoyable journey and the outcomes have been flowing through to our day to day business. Thanks Rob.

Daniel Crawford – General Manager, Hallam Truck Centre

Robert has been working with us for the past two years assisting us with business coaching and strategic planning. He has really helped us engage our team better and to be better able to look at key metrics in our organisation to drive financial performance. Rob is great to work with.

Erik Birzulis – Managing Director, Landair Surveys

Rob has been actively involved in helping me elevate the operating model across three businesses now. Rob's facilitation, mentoring, coaching and general advice provides significant value as he asks the hard questions, challenges one's thinking and stresses focus on executing the 'top 5' as you embark on your strategic journey. Rather than just an external consultant I see Rob as very much part of the team. If you are looking at scaling your business and are willing to be challenged, I could not recommend Rob highly enough.

Ross Gallagher – Executive General Manager, Home Care, IRT Group

When Rob was introduced to Dimple we were entering a phase of significant change and growth. Rob quickly built rapport and became a trusted ally to all our leaders. He could play the role as both the constructive devil's advocate and then pivot and be that positive catalyst to generate new ideas. His methods always made sure our team was kicking at the same goal and moving faster than we could alone. The business grew strategically and profitably, culminating in an outstanding sale to a public company. I strongly believe trust is earned through the consistent demonstration of both great character and competence. Rob has oodles of both! Rob Nankervis is a rock star… and more importantly, a valued and trusted friend.

Nick Beckett – Consultant and Strategic Advisor, ex-CEO of Dimple and T2

Rob has been an incredible asset to Bounce. His breadth of knowledge and real world experience have given us greater clarity and understanding as we scale. We have not only gained insight into what we need to do, but how we do it. We have seen a benefit to our own growth as a company along with seeing fantastic results with the engagement of our staff in this process.

Maria Smith – CEO and Founder, Bounce Australia

Our business was forty years old and solid, but it was a good time for a refresh: we wanted to grow, to make that growth more profitable and to keep the business easy to run as we scaled. With Rob's guidance we established a multi-year strategic plan and implemented execution disciplines of priority-setting, metrics and meeting rhythms. We had a strong boost to profit in our first year and, within a couple of years, had attracted a European buyer. Rob has been by our side through numerous changes, helping us to develop the clarity and alignment to navigate the challenges and opportunities. I would recommend him to other leaders seeking to boost growth and performance.

James Agius – Managing Director, ECOTECH Pty Ltd

Rob has been a vital member of our strategic planning team and the team feels like he is part of the business. As a group we have a regular annual/quarterly cadence for planning out of which UCS has grown in excess of thirty per cent per year for the last two years as we execute our strategic plan. This is a credit to the excellent team/culture at UCS, and equally that Rob's guidance and support has materially contributed to our growth story. UCS will be maintaining our successful relationship with Rob for the foreseeable future and I would recommend him to any company that wants to grow, develop and thrive.

Stephen Ellich – CEO and Managing Director, UCS Group

After many years of conducting strategic planning sessions without any real follow through I decided it was time for some external help. Rob guided us through strategic planning using a comprehensive system which really forced us to look hard into where we were and where we wanted to be. Importantly we engaged Rob for follow up sessions that brought our team accountability to deliver. Our ability to plan and execute strategy has improved dramatically along with a corresponding sense of purpose and team cohesion. I can highly recommend Rob for any organisation wanting to improve their strategic planning and execution capabilities.

Nicholas Dal Sasso – Owner, ECOTECH Pty Ltd

Rob's approach makes him not only enjoyable to work with, but helps so much in challenging times when change is needed to scale one's business. His knowledge of the market has been so well matched that we have seen great changes within the business, particularly focusing on the activities we need to nail to get the team results we are wanting. Thanks Rob!!

Nyree Hibberd – Owner, Koh Living

Growing a business is like scaling Mount Everest. There are various stages as we go up. Mountaineers have to adjust their approach after each stage because temperatures plummet, oxygen is insufficient and the seriousness of consequences increases. As business owners, if we can't adapt to the mounting challenges as we grow, our current stage becomes the peak, limiting our ambitions and constraining our true potential. Accordingly, we must adjust our approach as our enterprises grow if we wish to continue moving towards the top. I'm incredibly proud to say our team scaled our particular Mount Everest and I know we couldn't have got there without Rob Nankervis' seasoned guidance.

Damien James – Founder, Dimple

Judging by the types of organisations that work with Rob Nankervis, it becomes pretty clear, pretty quickly, that he really is the man to talk to about scaling a business. His book, *Propelling Performance*, showcases both his depth of knowledge on business growth as well as his passion to help business owners and managers to achieve their performance goals, no matter how big and hairy they may be. An impressive man, a great writer and without a doubt, a leader in this space.

Andrew Griffiths – International Bestselling Author and Global Speaker

I have had the great pleasure of working with Rob in coach training workshops and have seen him in action on several occasions. He truly has mastered the art of coaching and consistently makes an immediate, positive impact on all those with whom he interacts. Rob is always on….in service of his clients. He sees every conversation as an opportunity to help the other person gain valuable insights, become inspired, assume personal accountability and take concerted action. Uniquely, he sees himself not so much as a consultant but, rather, as a catalyst helping individuals and teams perform at their very best.

Gregg Thompson – President, Bluepoint Leadership Development. Author: *The Master Coach*

First published in 2020 by Robert Nankervis

© Robert Nankervis 2020
The moral rights of the author have been asserted

All rights reserved. Except as permitted under the *Australian Copyright Act 1968* (for example, a fair dealing for the purposes of study, research, criticism or review), no part of this book may be reproduced, stored in a retrieval system, communicated or transmitted in any form or by any means without prior written permission.

All inquiries should be made to the author.

A catalogue entry for this book is available from the National Library of Australia.

ISBN: 978-1-922391-21-6

Project management and text design by Publish Central
Cover design by Peter Reardon

Disclaimer: The material in this publication is of the nature of general comment only, and does not represent professional advice. It is not intended to provide specific guidance for particular circumstances and it should not be relied on as the basis for any decision to take action or not take action on any matter which it covers. Readers should obtain professional advice where appropriate, before making any such decision. To the maximum extent permitted by law, the author and publisher disclaim all responsibility and liability to any person, arising directly or indirectly from any person taking or not taking action based on the information in this publication.

Contents

This book is dedicated to my family, for their love and support,
and to the many business leaders I've met who strive every day
to do things better for their families, their teams and their clients,
and in so doing become the best version of themselves.

Foreword

I first met Rob Nankervis at a public Scaling Up event I ran in Australia – he was keen to learn the techniques to help the professional services firm that he part-owned.

Fast forward a decade and Rob is a leading Coach in our global cohort of Scaling Up Certified Coaches, a member of my Global Advisory Board, and he became the first Coach in Australia to run regular public workshops when I stepped down from that role. He has now engaged hundreds of leaders in the Scaling Up methodology – the same approach that Glen Richards, Naomi Simson, and Scott Farquhar have used and endorsed to grow their remarkable businesses at Greencross, Red Balloon and Atlassian respectively.

Rob is an avid learner and generous in sharing his thoughts – he regularly shares valuable ideas with me and the Coach community, in speaking engagements and on social media, and he's also written his *Rob's Insights* column, sharing ideas with his readership since 2014.

Now, in *Propelling Performance* he's bringing together his three decades of learning and experience and drawing on the proven approaches of thought leaders such as Jim Collins, Patrick Lencioni, Brad Smart and myself. It's a practical reflection of Rob's approach to helping his coaching clients to drive performance, accelerate growth and build value in their mid-tier businesses.

If your business is stuck and you don't know what to do about it, Rob will show you how to find your purpose, develop your strategy, set goals, attract and keep the right people, lead your team, measure your progress and much more. His 'three-sphere model' breaks his process into easy-to-follow steps.

Many businesses remain in mediocrity as they make the same mistakes over and over, trying to use the same thinking that began the stall to get them moving again. And an underperforming business drains energy and enthusiasm from your team, making it even more difficult to move forward.

Leading a business out of this trap is difficult. Rob has helped hundreds of businesses and leaders, and he can help you too.

I hope you enjoy and learn from Rob's journey to get your business out of its stall and propel it to even higher performance.

Verne Harnish, Founder, Gazelles, Scaling Up and EO.
Author: *Scaling Up*, *The Greatest Business Decisions of All Time* and *Mastering the Rockefeller Habits*

Introduction

'Only three things happen naturally in organisations: friction, confusion, and underperformance. Everything else requires leadership.'

Peter Drucker, management theorist

If you're like most of the leaders I meet you are probably the founder, owner or a senior leader in what most observers would call 'a good business'. You've been in business for a while and produce a good standard of products and services. Things tick along, the customers are served, the bills get paid.

At the same time, though, you notice that others in your network (or in the press) seem to be booming, and you have a sense that things have stalled. With everything that has been put in place – the team, the infrastructure, the investment in products, the systems, and the energy you've personally contributed – you feel it should really be lifting now, not just rolling along. It's very frustrating.

As a coach, adviser and a speaker at business events, here's what I've noticed: I'm meeting smart, driven, capable people who feel stuck. I see the impact on them personally – they know that their business could be so much more, and they're carrying a heavy load. For some it's a load steeped in the history of family ownership and obligation, for others it's the financial or status expectations of their business partners or spouse, while for others it's completely self-inflicted.

And the whole world of 'better, faster, cheaper' and bombardment of ideas doesn't make things easier – it just adds to the pressure and confusion: get a better CRM, shift the factory offshore, increase staff flexibility, Uber-ise our business model ... I've heard lots of them and I know you'll have your own list.

Truth is we know we need to do *something* to drive the performance, growth and value of our business ... but what ... and how ... and where do we start?

I faced the same challenges myself when I first became a leader and wished I'd had the guidance. And as I grew through my commercial career I became an observer of businesses and leaders where I worked and consulted and have continued to read widely about what works and doesn't. Now a professional coach, adviser and speaker, I'm a passionate student of business and leadership.

While I don't specifically know your business, I've worked with all sorts of businesses – professional firms, food and agricultural producers, manufacturers, healthcare providers, wholesalers, retailers, industrial and commercial services, to name just a few – so I know that business or industry type is not the challenge. The real challenge is that we have blockages in one or more of the critical energy centres in our business, and they are constraining or draining its spiritual, intellectual and physical energy.

But it doesn't need to be that way.

I've worked out that there are three fundamental 'spheres of energy' that you need to build and balance in your business and they capture what you believe, what you conceive and what you achieve. These energy spheres are complemented by three propeller blades that help move the energy from one sphere to the next delivering aspiration, activation and escalation. The central spindle around which all this activity flows is leadership, as it is the leader's role to control the pace and energy flow in the business. Think of the role as Chief Energy Officer rather than Chief Executive Officer.

Before we move on, I want to acknowledge the elephant in the room: with some of the concepts I'll share I expect there may be a sense of 'I've heard all this before'. But I also expect that much of what you've heard or read so far has lacked context and therefore created more mental clutter. One of my key insights is that there is a relatively small set of principles that support business success – but there is an order to them that makes a significant difference. And that's what I'll be sharing with you.

Imagine what life would be like if you could get those blocks out of the way.

I'll share my many years of experience, my ideas and the principles that sit behind them, some principles and practices I've learned from other thought leaders, and stories from my clients and other successful businesses. But this book is about you, helping you to recognise and remove your blocks, and take those necessary actions to propel your performance.

THE PROBLEM

Get on any peak-hour train, bus or tram, or even look around at your fellow passengers in an airline business lounge, or stuck in peak-hour traffic. Look at the faces. I've been doing this, and what I see bothers me. I see little joy, energy or passion on its way to work. That's bad news for you as a leader, because some of these people could be on your team; and it's bad news for the rest of us, because we're probably being served by them when we deal with your business.

If you look again on the way home, you'll find their expressions have hardly changed. The plus is that, as a leader, you haven't made them any worse (today, anyway), but they're no better either.

The reason: they work in energy-sucking, underperforming businesses.

It's little wonder that the majority of our businesses don't work the way we would like. Few employees are inspired by their work and their business and, if we are the leader, that condition is down to us.

Why is this happening? I believe it's an energy management issue. For a start, I believe most businesses lack a sense of purpose to which their staff can connect and a set of strong values to which people can subscribe. Today's workplace, it seems, is founded more on policy and less on passion. Further, in a directional sense, faddism has taken over from common sense. Rather than focusing on a thoughtfully constructed medium-term plan, businesses bounce from one quick-fix strategy to another. One year it's mergers and acquisitions, the next it's an organisational restructure, then business process reengineering or implementing the latest technology or new product. When none of this works, businesses often decide one or more of the leaders is the issue, quickly put someone new in their place, and start the whole process over again.

This is compounded by the sense that, whatever you do in today's economy, the results should be *fast*. At the top end of town, corporate analysts and the media continue to demand higher performance in shorter times. Boards then get sucked into short-term incentives to drive 'the right behaviours'. Inevitably, these approaches and expectations cascade down to the mid-tier firms. Rather than doing the work required to put solid foundations in place, businesses today are reactionary, searching for the next big thing that will give them a miraculous breakthrough.

This is where most businesses lose propulsion and begin their stall. By lurching back and forth from idea to idea, these businesses never build the clarity, alignment and momentum necessary for growth. They never create a clear vision or become known in their industry. And this results in a downward spiral where every failed new initiative has a detrimental impact on the momentum built up in the previous push, along with the time and resources invested in that push. Lacklustre growth becomes flat performance which, left unchecked, becomes negative growth and the business continues to struggle or fails entirely, its value eroded or decimated.

Finally, because there is such a fluctuating cluster of initiatives, leaders and external circumstances, there is no clear understanding of or connection to what really went wrong … or knowledge of whether anything went wrong at all. The leaders then wonder, 'Are we really any worse than the rest? Perhaps this is just the current market.' True or not, the good ones know that they are well behind where they should be, and that much of the turbulence they feel was self-inflicted.

Ultimately, this means that over time strong-performing people don't want to work for these businesses, customers don't want to buy from them, and the seeds of failure are sown.

Happily for most, changes in the economy, gyrations of market valuations, the competitive pressures of the sector, and a rotation of leaders will conspire to provide enough fog so that most businesses can explain away their sub-optimal performance.

If, on the other hand, you're ready to *solve* your business's performance issues, rather than simply ignoring, disguising or excusing them, read on.

THE SOLUTION

If you look to the natural environment, none of the strong, enduring features, such as tropical rainforests or coral reefs, came about quickly. They formed incrementally, and with a great deal of effort on Mother Nature's behalf.

The same goes for great businesses.

Rare 'unicorn' business aside, when you go behind the scenes of great businesses, in most cases you will discover that enduring growth builds up over time (such as one of my clients, in its fourth generation of family leaders after eighty-five years). While a 'tip of the iceberg' transformation may have looked quick, dramatic or revolutionary from the outside, within the business it was a result of having strong, purposeful foundations, strategically building on these and following through with persistent, aligned actions.

Each aligned action these businesses took built momentum. This growing momentum led to visible results. These results energised their people to take *more* action and 'suddenly', through taking targeted, consistent, persistent steps, these businesses were operating in a positive, self-reinforcing upward cycle.

In my work as a business consultant, adviser and executive coach, I meet with the leaders of companies of a range of sizes in a variety of industries to lead them through the steps to take their business to the next level. My method is drawn from my own professional experience over the last thirty-five years being exposed to a plethora of business types, sizes and ownership structures. As an auditor, accountant, project leader, head hunter, director and owner, and more recently as a business and executive coach, I have had the good fortune to observe at close quarters what works and doesn't. Regardless of a business's size, sector or lifecycle stage, there are commonalities to success. I've uncovered the common threads, principles and fundamental practices that need to be addressed in any business seeking better performance, growth and valuation. I've distilled the elements into a model for business transformation.

My goal was to create a model for success for my clients, many of whom are, in a sense, 'accidental' business leaders. They were fantastic at the functional 'thing' that they began their career doing, got some more people and products and services around them, progressively won some bigger clients and then, after many years of solid effort, found themselves at the helm of a significant operation.

MY THREE-SPHERE MODEL

One of the great privileges of my work is coaching clients to make the necessary changes within their business to help it reach its full potential. I do this with what I call my 'three-sphere' model. This involves three core areas of energy management for a business and its leaders: the emotional, intellectual and physical. It is through being constructive in the development and application of these energies that leaders influence what they believe, what they conceive and what they achieve within their business.

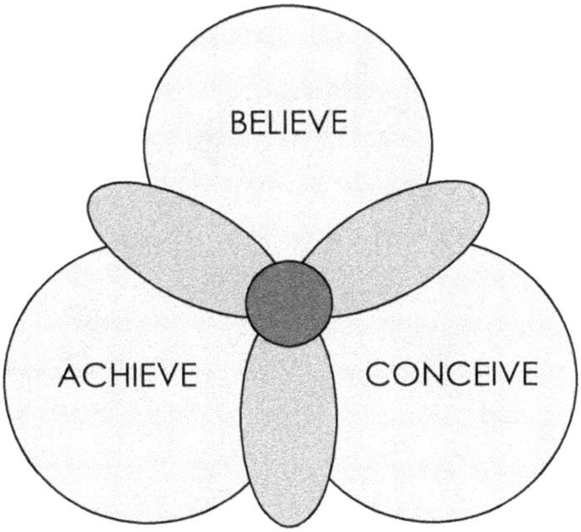

Believe

Believe – the first 'sphere' in the above model – covers the foundations that every high-growth business creates before reaching a sustained breakthrough, and includes your business's purpose, values and vision. Nailing this piece of the puzzle will both *direct* everything you do as well as *fuel* everything you do, providing the emotional/spiritual energy and resilience to keep your business moving forward while absorbing the knocks along the way.

When you get this right, you will discover that the energy created by your purpose, values and vision is contagious. It acts like a magnet, drawing in likeminded staff, customers and partners who are just as committed to making your business a success as you, providing the key to building momentum. Representing how people *feel*, it also acts as the guiding light or spirit of your business, informing the 'thinking and doing' aspects.

Conceive

In this stage, things get more concrete. Informed by the guiding principles provided by the *Believe* stage, the *Conceive* sphere focuses on creating the strategy and business model to achieve your vision and ultimately live your purpose. This part represents how you *think* about the business; drawing out its intellectual energy.

Businesses that don't tackle this stage will drift. They have lower focus, and tend to behave reactively, only addressing the challenges that get thrown their way rather than working towards a shared goal. These businesses are also exposed to higher risk, simply because they haven't taken the time to consider possible risks and create a strategy to mitigate them. They can also become misaligned with customer needs, generally being more attached to their product or service than to actually creating value for their customers.

However, if you get this stage right, your business will have a clear roadmap to achieve your goal and align with your purpose, values and vision.

Achieve

Many businesses make the mistake of creating big plans to achieve big goals, but don't consider the processes, structures and people required to implement them. This results in frustrated staff who are overworked, torn between competing priorities and unable to do their best work; constantly changing strategies to work around resourcing issues and clumsy processes; and the financial struggles that flow on from these unending directional changes. Energy is dissipated.

The *Achieve* sphere avoids those issues by putting in place the pieces you need to implement your strategy effectively – it's about getting clear on what you *do*. This includes enabling the right processes, creating the right organisational structure, and populating it with the right people. Once you have these pieces in place, your business will be focused on the activities that are the most highly aligned and profitable, and your people will be empowered to get the most important pieces of work done and done well. Friction decreases and momentum starts to build.

THE WHITE SPACE

But there is more to this model than just the three spheres of energy. My experience has shown that it's the white space around and connecting these ideas – and what takes place in here – that will drive you towards success or failure.

Between each sphere there needs to be some sort of mechanism or connective tissue to link one idea to the next. Recognising these connective elements helps ensure that your business and the people within it work on these enablers by creating a clear, interdependent relationship between them. Indeed, the lack of understanding and consideration of these connectors is a key source of underperformance.

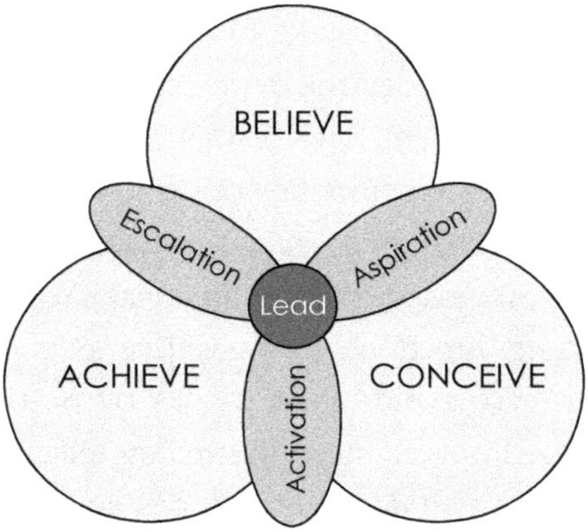

Aspiration connects the *Believe* stage to the *Conceive* stage. It's about making your purpose, values and vision concrete so they can inform your business strategy. And the best way I've found to do this is with what business author Jim Collins termed a 'BHAG': a big, hairy, audacious goal.[1] Once you've gained clarity on your own ambitions, the other important aspiration to consider is that of your customer – what are *they* trying to get done? Then, to ground these aspirations in reality, what is the capability of your organisation to deliver on all of this? In short, this section draws out 'what do we really want?'

Activation is how you connect your strategy, the *Conceive* stage, to your business and the changes that need to occur to implement the strategy (the *Achieve* stage). During *Activation*, you translate your

---

1 Jim Collins, *Good to Great: Why some companies make the leap… and others don't* (New York: Harper Collins Publishers, 2001), 197.

thinking into action by communicating your strategy with your people. As they will be carrying it out, the way your team receives this strategy will be a demonstration of their commitment. At this stage, it is also critical to be clear about accountability for delivering on the agreed priorities, and to declare the measures that will track progress. This part answers the question 'what is most important?'

Escalation connects the actions taken by your business and people to what you *Believe*. Rejoicing in the achievements puts energy back into your business and reinforces those beliefs, which ensures they continue to inform business decisions. Reflection on success and failure allows you to extract important learnings to position your business for its next upward spiral. It's then time for a reset that takes the learnings from what we've already achieved, holds them up against where we're headed, and guides us to the next set of choices. We're building a cadence where the more things continue to go right, the more positive reinforcement goes through the business, the more valuable the business becomes, and the easier it is to move from strength to strength. It sets you up to define the next stage of your growth quest. You avoid getting stuck. This part answers the question 'what's next?'

These elements act like the blades of a propeller, pushing each of the three spheres towards higher levels of performance … hence, the model for *Propelling Performance*.

THE FINAL PIECE

The final piece of the propeller, dead centre, is *Leadership*. Leaders are the people who help connect and energise all of the spheres and ensure the blades keep turning.

Leadership is the critical spindle that drives the success of the propeller model. Leaders help guide speed of delivery and the power it generates, thus dictating the altitude to which your business ascends, how fast that journey is, and how smooth the ride. Leaders drive the process of making ethereal beliefs into sensible, tangible concepts and decisions, which can then be executed. Without strong leaders, all of the other pieces in the model remain theory, rather than practice, and your business will struggle to adapt and grow. Great leaders practise all three crucial elements: leading themselves, leading their team and leading the business. This final part challenges leaders with the question 'who do I need to be?'

WHAT TO EXPECT

I believe in making businesses great places to work. People not only spend a substantial part of their lives at work, they also seek self-expression and fulfilment through serving others. In doing so, they grow their clients, themselves and their business. It is our obligation as leaders, then, to create the right environment for this growth and to make it an enjoyable and fulfilling experience.

Businesses that don't address the fundamentals will remain stuck. Yes, they may have an occasional lucky moment or breakthrough but, because they don't have the fundamentals in place, any spike in growth isn't sustainable and therefore won't add to the longer-term success or valuation of the business. At best they stagnate, failing to live up to their promise or potential, and many will fall backwards.

By contrast, the businesses that *do* address these fundamentals see outstanding results. By following my model, I've seen clients achieve double-digit revenue growth, drive substantial profit increases, and turn their teams towards high performance, all while making their business easier to manage and much more valuable. Others have seen it through to very successful exits.

Your business can achieve the same.

So, to get the most out of this book, I recommend the following:

1. Take notes in the book as you read. If you saw my library you'd notice that the books are peppered with annotated sticky notes – it's a great aid to remembering and also to finding the information again.
2. Where I prompt you with questions throughout the book, take the time to consider an answer. For some of the questions, if you have a team, you may wish to ask them for their insights.
3. Throughout the book are dotted 'Propeller tips'. These are largely drawn from my in-house work with clients and are ideas they've found useful. So, if you're not already doing these things you should actively consider them.
4. When reviewing the key points at the end of each chapter, reflect on whether this is an area you now understand sufficiently or if you need to dig deeper.
5. Set aside some time for the 'Take Action' sections, where I prompt you with five questions to close out each chapter.

You already have a good business, so let's build on that foundation to make its growth, performance and value everything you know it can be.

Let's get started.

PART I
Believe

'The companies that survive longest are the ones that work out what they uniquely can give to the world – not just growth or money but their excellence, their respect for others, or their ability to make people happy. Some call those things a soul.'

Charles Handy, philosopher and business author

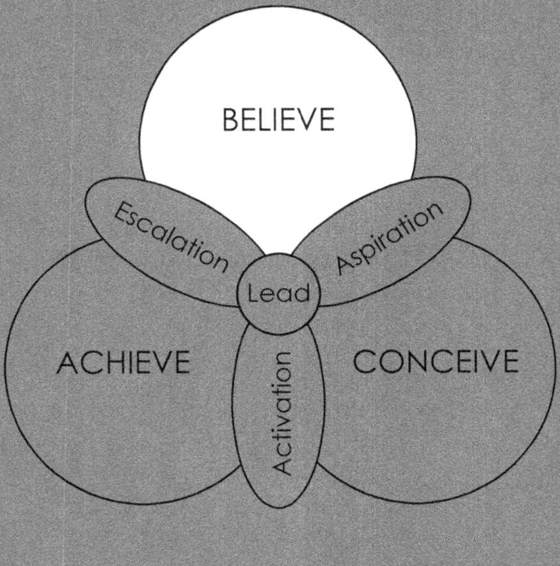

BELIEVE covers the foundations that every high-growth business creates before reaching a sustained breakthrough, including your business's purpose, values and vision. Nailing this piece of the puzzle will both *direct* everything you do as well as *fuel* everything you do, providing the energy and resilience to keep your business moving forward while absorbing the inevitable knocks along the way.

Representing how people *feel*, it also acts as the guiding light, heart or spirit of your business, informing the subsequent 'thinking and doing' aspects. It answers the question: 'who are we?'

CHAPTER 1

Purpose

'Purpose turns out to be the quality that CEOs most need in order to do their jobs well. Purpose is the difference between good and great, between honourable success and legendary performance, between fifteen minutes of fame and a legacy.'

Nikos Mourkogiannis, CEO and author

THE IMPORTANCE OF A CLEAR PURPOSE

At 6 am the alarm starts beeping. Most people groan, hit snooze and doze for another ten (or thirty) minutes.

When they eventually rise, they rub the sleep from their eyes and shuffle to the shower, limbs heavy and mind foggy. They shuffle out of the shower, into their clothes, and into the office. Everything feels like it's too much and they do the bare minimum to get by.

Occasionally they'll commit to a motivating goal, but in a few weeks they run out of steam and return to the status quo.

By contrast, the most successful people in the world are often up at 5 am. They bound out of bed with determination and enthusiasm for their day. They have already meditated, exercised and set their goals for the day by the time most people are eating their cereal.

What's the difference between these two types of people?

The most successful people are driven by a higher purpose. This gives them energy, motivation and determination every day to do whatever it takes to live that purpose. This makes them strong enough to weather the difficult times, innovative enough to recognise and leverage opportunities, and organised enough to make it happen.

Your business works in the same way – it's the sum of all the purposes and efforts that get brought to work each day.

Your purpose is *why* you do what you do. It's the 'we believe' or 'we are here to' statement that encapsulates why your business exists, which then becomes a guiding light for the 'what', 'how', 'who' and 'when' that turn your beliefs into tangible outcomes. It's the reason for your business's existence beyond simply making money, and it allows your people to collectively accomplish something much greater than what they could achieve on their own.

SOME EXAMPLES OF A CLEAR PURPOSE

Companies with a clear purpose that drives business decisions and actions can achieve extraordinary results. Take, for instance, the inspired decision by Australians Simon Griffiths, Jehan Ratnatunga and Danny Alexander to start Who Gives a Crap (WGAC), a toilet paper company that is also a social enterprise, helping to build toilets for those in need. The company was launched in July 2012 when Simon Griffiths made the unorthodox decision to sit on a toilet in a draughty warehouse, refusing to move until they had raised enough pre-orders to start production of their toilet paper. 'Fifty hours and one cold bottom later' they'd raised over $50,000 through a crowd-funding campaign.[1]

Simon's toilet vigil fascinated the community at large and thousands of people watched his live-feed video. The fledgling company received media attention from around the globe, all for a guy sitting on a toilet for something he believed in. This passion in turn

1 au.whogivesacrap.org/pages/about-us

attracted a legion of fans who were captivated by the quirky, socially responsible start-up and their purpose.

From the outset, the directors offered transparency and authenticity about how their purpose would support their goals. They would donate fifty per cent of profits to carefully chosen charity partners such as WaterAid Australia; organisations with deep experience and skill in implementing high-impact sanitation projects throughout the developing world. The other half of the profits would be put into the business to ultimately build more toilets.

WGAC also addresses the issue surrounding traditional production methods of toilet paper: environmental impact. WGAC products are made from recycled paper, and each roll is also individually wrapped in paper, with a unique, fun design. The product arrives via home delivery, in a box with a thank you message.

To date WGAC has donated over $1.8 million to charity 'and saved a heck of a lot of trees, water and energy'. They have expanded their product range from simply 'TP' to paper towels and facial tissues.

The 'why' behind Who Gives a Crap has attracted a legion of loyal fans: 'We love toilet paper because for us, it's our way of making a difference. We started Who Gives A Crap when we learnt that 2.3 billion people across the world don't have access to a toilet. That's roughly forty per cent of the global population and means that around 289,000 children under five die every year from diarrhoeal diseases caused by poor water and sanitation. That's almost 800 children per day, or one child every two minutes. We thought that was pretty crap.'

The company has made it easy for people who want an opportunity 'to do something for the world' – and in doing so, tapped into each person's 'why'. What's more, they automatically 'employed' thousands of people who were willing to promote their product – for free.

To communicate their unique 'why', WGAC uses marketing messages that are humorous, irreverent and always involve toilet humour. Their regular email campaigns feature cute animal videos. They schedule special-themed print runs of packaging for Christmas. Their website features phrases such as, 'Delivered to your door. Well, your front door. To your bathroom would be creepy', and, 'Stop wiping with trees! Buy 100 per cent recycled toilet paper.'

Consumers loved the fact that WGAC made the topic of toilet paper (TP) and toilet humour mainstream. Within months, excited customers adopted the cheeky style of WGAC and began photographing their delivery of TP, often with their pets, and building TP towers and creations and posting to social media.

It's just one example of how a genuine 'why' can transcend the norm and become a customer 'why', too. They are joining a cause, rather than just transacting business.

The team behind WGAC not only live their purpose and values, but achieve something even bigger. They make a sustainable impact in line with the UN Sustainable Development Goals. WGAC's commitment to building toilets has a direct impact on improved sanitation (Goal 6) and health (Goal 3).

WGAC is only one of several Australian start-ups with an impressive and admirable approach to living their purpose. Thank You is a social enterprise founded in 2009, that commits one hundred per cent of profit to ending global poverty. From a bottle of water created to help end the world water crisis, their idea has grown to over fifty-five products, from personal care to nappies and baby care. Thank You now contributes to goal 1 (End Poverty), goal 3 (Health) and goal 5 (Gender Equality).

Another Melbourne start-up, Zero Impact, has invented a natural fuel from recycled coffee grounds, with a plan to reduce emissions and change our carbon footprint (goal 12). Zero Impact founder

Max Middleweek was the brains behind the 'Briki', a briquette made of highly compressed coffee grounds that makes firewood redundant. The Briki has the potential for significant impact, reusing grounds from some of the six billion cups of coffee that go to landfill every year, break down into methane gas and accelerate climate change.

Each of the small teams behind WGAC, Thank You and Zero Impact began with belief, passion and highly defined values that ensure they never lose sight of the bigger picture – and neither do their customers, who know their purchase has a direct impact for the planet. The success of such companies speaks for itself – and is due to the potency of a strong guiding purpose.

If you don't have a clear purpose as the leader, and your business doesn't have a clear purpose, it is effectively operating as a soulless machine. While the machine might function well for a time, machines generally don't build lasting loyalty among your team or clients. Lower staff and customer engagement will follow, according to Gallup research.[2] Only a third of the US workforce strongly agreed that their corporate mission or purpose made them feel that their job was important, while brands without aligned purposes and brand promises only win half the share of wallet (twenty-three per cent) as brands with such alignment (forty-seven per cent).

Ultimately, if you don't have a strong purpose, your customers are likely to act transactionally, and you'll notice them shopping around as they look for the best price. Disloyal staff and disengaged customers mean your business is left fighting both internal and external battles and starts acting from a reactive space rather than a strategic one.

But when you *do* get it right, you'll find that your business noticeably has more energy, energy that will fuel everything you do. This energy is contagious, as you probably felt from the case studies

---

2 Nate Dvorak and Bryant Ott, 'A Company's Purpose Has to Be a Lot More Than Words', *Gallup Workplace*, July 28, 2015. gallup.com/businessjournal/184376/company-purpose-lot-words.aspx.

I shared earlier, and a business that nails this will start to act like a magnet. It will draw in the right staff, the right customers and the right opportunities. In turn, these people, customers and opportunities will start to attract *more* of the right people, customers and opportunities, and momentum continues to build as your business moves from strength to strength.

THE VERSATILITY OF A CLEAR PURPOSE

A clear purpose also allows your business to be versatile. We can see this working in purpose-driven companies like Apple that have branched into, and succeeded in, multiple industries.

As marketing expert Simon Sinek discusses in his highly influential book *Start with Why*, most companies talk about *what* they do – the product or service they deliver. If Apple marketed in this way, their pitch might be, 'We make great computers. They're beautifully designed, simple to use and user-friendly. Wanna buy one?'[3]

This is the way most businesses communicate. There's nothing wrong with this. Typically, they are speaking the truth – they do have great products and there is some factor that differentiates them from everyone else in the marketplace. But if you're focusing on the *product* rather than the *purpose behind the product*, you will forever be tied to that product rather than making a deeper connection.

This is the reason that, rather than starting with *what*, Apple starts with *why*. This ethos has been summed up by Sinek as:

> *'Everything we do, we believe in challenging the status quo. We believe in thinking differently. The way we challenge the status quo is by making our products beautifully designed, simple to use*

3 Simon Sinek, *Start with Why: How great leaders inspire everyone to take action* (New York: Penguin, 2009), 40.

> *and user friendly. We just happen to make great computers. Wanna buy one?'*[4]

People subscribe to the *why* or the purpose of a company, not the *what* or the product. And this is why people queue to buy computers from Apple, along with music players and phones, and pay a premium to own them. You've convinced the customer to join a cause, rather than simply transact. An emotional connection has been made.

By having a clear purpose, Apple has become more than just another computer company. This has given it a branding edge over competitors throughout its history. Look no further than when Dell launched its own music players in 2003. Dell was still seen as a computer company, and buying a music player from a computer company felt incongruent. Sales figures reflected the disconnect, and before long the product was discontinued. On the other hand, buying a music player from a company that was challenging the status quo was compelling because, by buying that product, the customers could align themselves with a brand they felt was at the forefront of innovation.

By making its purpose about something greater than the products it sells at any given time, Apple has been able to successfully diversify in an ever-changing digital sphere.

THE DRIVING FORCE OF YOUR BUSINESS

The ultimate benefit of a strong purpose, however, is that it will become the driving force behind all decisions you make as a business. It will inform your strategy. It will help you decide who you should hire and who you shouldn't. It helps motivate your employees and

4 Simon Sinek, *Start with Why: How great leaders inspire everyone to take action* (New York: Penguin, 2009), 41.

build morale, as they feel their work is worthwhile. It will help you choose the right partners, as they need to believe what you believe.

Several years ago, when I worked in executive search, I was retained by a leading Australian religious-based health service to find a new CEO who was aligned with the organisation's purpose, which was to serve and advocate for marginalised clients.

From the interviewed shortlist of leading candidates, the Board agreed on the preferred candidate who had the highest capability and experience required for the position. At this point, a special governance group was brought into the process for the final vetting. This small senior group had the power of a go/no-go decision based solely on the candidate's fit with their organisational mission.

In the five years that I worked in executive search, this was the only business I encountered that made their purpose so central to everything they did, including hiring. This organisation overtly hired based on alignment to their mission, vision and values. This action spoke volumes to the integrity of their commitment and compassion for the poor and vulnerable.

Furthermore, their belief system underpinned their standard of care and business model, which has seen them remain a successful not-for-profit across all their services to this day. The strategic growth that they plan is also founded in service of their faith and to expand their aid to those in need.

It's clear to see that a fully realised and integrated purpose will not only attract the right people to your organisation, it also helps drive strategy and growth.

WHAT ARE MOST BUSINESSES DOING WRONG?

I know … none of this is new. In fact, so many leaders are discussing the importance of having a clear purpose today that it's starting to feel like just another fad. And yet, so many businesses are still missing this crucial element, which should in fact be central to everything they do. Most organisations simply don't have a purpose, or a clearly espoused purpose.

Meanwhile, other businesses *say* they have a purpose, however it isn't creating the inspiration and drive that a purpose should. In such cases the 'purpose' is simply a phrase that the marketing team has developed to use in press releases or on the website. Other businesses simply describe their current product lines or customer segments as a purpose. In neither of these instances does the 'purpose' truly answer the question of *why* the business does what it does.

A lack of purpose, the wrong purpose, or even a useful purpose that has not been clearly communicated or embedded into the life of your organisation creates a situation where the only default purpose for your stakeholders, your staff and your customers is money. Your stakeholders want a higher return, your staff want better salaries and your customers want better deals. This results in uninspired staff, disloyal customers and weak partnerships.

From a strategic point of view, the major departments in your business will constantly call for new strategies, thinking *that* will be the solution. However, when these strategies meet with implementation issues, the focus turns towards major structural change as the solution. In other words, the default is to look first towards action, before testing for congruence and alignment.

The truth is that all of these are Band-Aid solutions, and they are doomed to fail if you don't build the foundation of an aligning core purpose.

This is the reason why businesses that otherwise seem to do everything 'right' (choosing the right people, creating the right processes, creating a sound strategy, and more) *still* don't get the results they want.

So if purpose is so important, and we *know* it's so important, why do so many businesses struggle to get it right, or avoid it entirely?

It's because a purpose is conceptual. Unlike a task, process, role or strategy, all of which can be defined and measured, a purpose cannot. It's difficult to directly attribute success to 'what your business believes'. As a result, most businesses choose to focus on the concrete elements such as people, structures and strategy instead. They can be written down and then tested and measured and put in a report.

HOW TO FIND YOUR PURPOSE

So, where should your business's purpose lie?

Often your external environment will influence your purpose. As Mourkogiannis says, 'The winner of corporate competition, at any given moment, is the company whose moral purpose best fits the prevailing environment and assets.'[5]

However, a 'purpose' that is based solely on external conditions will constantly change as those conditions change, and won't provide the steady foundation your business needs for growth. This is why I believe it's far more effective if your purpose comes from *you* rather than the market.

> *'A noble purpose inspires sacrifice, stimulates innovation and encourages perseverance.'*
>
> Gary Hamel, business author

The 'five whys' exercise

A powerful method for finding your business's purpose is the 'five whys' exercise.

5 Nikos Mourkogiannis, 'The Realist's Guide to Moral Purpose', *Strategy & Business*, November 29, 2005. strategy-business.com/article/05405.

Developed by Sakichi Toyoda and used as a part of Toyota's manufacturing methods, the five whys exercise was originally used for problem solving. According to the architect of the Toyota Production System, Taiichi Ohno, 'by repeating why five times, the nature of the problem as well as its solution becomes clear.'[6] Asking 'why' five times quickly got to the root cause of the problem, which meant Toyota could create a holistic solution, rather than simply treating one of the symptoms.

The five whys exercise is also a potent way to discover your business's purpose. Rather than starting with a problem, you start with a simple statement about what you do: the products you make, the services you deliver, or the customers you serve. Then ask 'why' five times.

Walmart's purpose isn't selling goods for low prices. Their purpose is the reason, or the *why*, behind those low prices – to give ordinary people the opportunity to buy the same products as the rich. Disney's purpose isn't about making cartoons or building theme parks. The *why* behind the cartoons and the theme parks is bringing happiness to millions.

Notice that neither of these purposes is about increasing profits or generating higher returns for their shareholders. The only people that 'higher shareholder returns' inspires are your shareholders. A true purpose, on the other hand, should inspire everyone who touches your business – staff, suppliers, customers and more. Profits and shareholder returns are the *result* of having a clear purpose, not the purpose itself.

So, what is *your* business's purpose?

---

6 Taiichi Ohno, *Toyota Production System: Beyond large-scale production* (Portland: Productivity Press, 1988), 123.

Simply start with a brief explanation of what your business does – the products you make, the services you deliver, or the customers you serve. Then ask yourself, why is that important? Why do you do it? Why was this business started?

Here's an example from doing this exercise with one of my clients who runs an IT company:

1. *Why do we provide managed IT services to our clients?* Because these systems are integral to their businesses.
2. *Why is it integral to our clients' businesses?* It helps them have reliability.
3. *Why is reliability important to them?* The data and systems that we support enable our clients to deliver on the expectations of their customers.
4. *Why is delivering on these expectations so important?* The clients can feel confidence and trust in the stability of their business.
5. *Why is this level of confidence and trust important to them?* So that they feel secure.

Once we'd finished this exercise, I took the client back to a conversation we'd had when they initially engaged me. They had spoken of their personal passion for helping orphans, and the commitment they were making to fund orphanages in the Asia-Pacific region. So now I was able to help them link their purpose back to their personal values – these guys were big believers in providing those around them with security. And yet they had never seen the congruence of this link until we brought it to the surface.

If you're struggling with the above exercise and think that defining a higher purpose is challenging in your industry, reflect on the purpose of building materials company Cemex. The one-hundred-year-old multinational firm turns over US$15 billion and operates in over fifty countries. Key to their enduring success was CEO Lorenzo Zambrano's ability to capture the imagination of his staff and customers with the assertion that this was not simply a commoditised cement producer. Their product 'means roads and hospitals, sewers, power plants, and water systems. For so many of our customers, cement is the stuff of dreams'. Further to the higher purpose of Cemex, he saw the firm as an ambassador for Mexico, and a symbol to her people that they can compete anywhere.[7] Powerful stuff.

Keep asking yourself *why* – after five whys, even if your purpose isn't word perfect, you should be getting close to articulating it.

One of my tests is that when you really hit the gold with this exercise you'll feel an emotion that really touches you and feels very authentic to what you're about. A note of caution though; while I was able to draw out the example above relatively quickly with my client, it is often a much more challenging exercise. Don't be surprised if you pick away at it over time until you get it right. With this, as with all the exercises that I recommend in this book, the final response won't necessarily tumble out in one sitting. That's okay – just keep coming back to it regularly, capturing key words or thoughts, and over time you'll see a pattern or essence of your purpose emerge.

PROPELLER TIP: Think back through the history of your business. Reflect on those moments where you've felt most proud. What was the contribution that was being made to someone outside the business? It's another hint to your 'why'.

---

7 Kerri A. Dolan, 'Lorenzo Zambrano: Thoughts on Business, Leadership, and Life', *Stanford Graduate School of Business*, May 19, 2014. gsb.stanford.edu/insights/lorenzo-zambrano-thoughts-business-leadership-life.

TESTING YOUR PURPOSE

Importantly, your business's purpose should generate a sense of commitment and pride for you and those in the team around you. This will foster a culture where employees are more motivated to go the extra mile to achieve better results in service of a greater good, rather than simply toiling away on day-in, day-out tasks.

Think of telling your children and other loved ones what your business does – would you feel proud describing your work in terms of the purpose you've defined?

How does this purpose make you feel? Does it energise and excite you? Or does it just feel like hollow PR-speak? Will this purpose be as valid in one hundred years' time as it is today? Or is it something you chose in response to market conditions?

Does this purpose help you think expansively about the long-term possibilities for your business, beyond its current products, services, markets, industries and strategies? Likewise, does this purpose help you to decide which activities to *not* pursue?

If you can answer all of these questions with a resounding *yes*, it's time to take this purpose to your staff, and then to your customers. Start to build it into your conversations and see if they have the same response.

Then, to keep your purpose alive, think about how it will be reflected in the regular activities of your business. Could the words and images in your communications, such as your website and other marketing collateral, speak more directly to your purpose? What about recruiting – how could the organisational purpose be woven into the process of finding and onboarding new talent? When making decisions within the business, are they serving your 'why'? Anything you do that increases the clarity and congruence of your actions with your beliefs is a step in the right direction.

One of my clients, UCS Group, has brought all this together nicely. Their purpose is 'Creating sustainable connected communities', and you can see it alive in the business. With staff, they have a focus on growing apprentices, which is not only a great contribution to the life of those young team members, it also makes UCS itself more sustainable through building and growing their own team. They also have at least four levels of leaders present at the Quarterly and Annual Reviews that I run, thereby involving lots of their talent in understanding how the business runs (keeping themselves sustainable). From a client perspective they have a strong service ethic to ensure that their projects get delivered safely, on time, first time to help the sustainability of their clients. Further, they've added a solar offering to enable sustainable power to the communities they serve. Finally, in the community, UCS likes to support the sustainability of the places in which they live and work, so they actively support local sports clubs and, during a substantial drought in Australia, contributed significantly to the 'Buy a Bale' campaign. A great example of bringing purpose to life and making it visible.

KEY POINTS

1. Purpose is critical. It underpins your business's energy and motivation. It is the driving force behind all decisions you make.
2. Your purpose is *why* you do what you do. It's the 'we believe' or 'we are here to' statement.
3. Most businesses do not have a clear purpose. They may be clear on *what* they do, but not *why*, which represents a weakness in their belief system.
4. A clear, well-crafted purpose will help you decide what to do and what *not* to do.
5. If your people and customers understand your purpose, the energy is contagious. The clarity and strength of your purpose will help attract more of the *right* people and opportunities.

TAKE ACTION

Do you know your purpose? If not, ask yourself the 'five whys'. Once you've defined it, ask yourself these questions:

1. What could you do to make your purpose more clear and authentic within your business? (Is it in your marketing, a key part of your recruiting, a guide to your decision-making?)
2. Does your purpose make you look at your own job differently? Will it make your employees and potential employees view their roles differently, enabling them to play a bigger game?
3. Is the purpose enduring? Will it be as valid in one hundred years as it is today?

4. Does this purpose help you think expansively about the long-term possibilities for your business? How would being more purposeful impact your strategy?
5. How could you connect daily activities more closely to your purpose?

CHAPTER 2

Values

'As far as the company is concerned,
the greatest thing [David Packard] left behind him
was a code of ethics known as the HP Way.'

Bill Hewlett, co-founder of Hewlett-Packard

SOME GREAT EXAMPLES OF COMPANY VALUES

When HP began over fifty years ago, it was founded on the basis of five values:

- trust and respect for individuals
- a focus on a high level of achievement and contribution
- conducting business with uncompromising integrity
- teamwork
- the encouragement of flexibility and innovation.

These values became the principles that guided everything that HP did – the HP Way.

Similarly, Australian-founded software company Atlassian is renowned for its values, which I regularly share as an example with my clients and event attendees.[1] The company catapulted from

1 Atlassian, 'The Value of Values', accessed November 11, 2014, atlassian.com/company/about/values.

start-up to a US$3.5 billion company in just twelve years, living the values of:

- embracing transparency at all levels, no matter how impractical
- caring about what they create
- treating their customers well (bluntly phrased as 'don't #@!% the customer' on their website)
- an emphasis on playing, as well as working, with the team
- being the change they seek in the world.

What does this look like in practice? The Atlassian Foundation espoused the original one per cent model – one per cent of Atlassian profits, one per cent of equity, one per cent of software licenses, and one per cent of employee time would be donated to non-profits. Today, the total amount donated to charity is just shy of US$4 million. On top of this, every full-time employee gets five days paid leave to work for their favourite non-profit. When it comes to having fun, the company has beer on tap, bean bags in the office, board meetings over board games, in-office yoga and in-office dogs. In turn, employees feel more positive about their work and have a stronger alignment with Atlassian's values. With this sort of coherence in place, the firm has ranked among Australia's best places to work for several years.

A client of mine, Dimple, the aged-care podiatry specialists, has also done the values piece very well. Through an exercise with the leadership team, we shaped the values into:

- do right
- be loved
- go beyond.

Importantly, these values are accompanied by *behaviours* that give a sense of 'what we'll see if these values are being lived'. In Dimple's case, the behavioural statement says: 'Do right stripped bare means we try to do what we say we will do. It's fairness personified. It's about committing, about being accountable and finding a place where everyone's voice feels heard.' Be loved says: 'You get what you put out there! To be loved means we have to give as well as take. It means we have been generous; with our time, spirit, smiles and laughs.' And finally, go beyond says: 'Our job descriptions are merely the starting point. Going beyond is doing the extra things to make someone's day, week, perhaps even year! We encourage everyone to actively look for better ways to do things and think how they can be the positive difference we want to see in the world.'

These are a great example of how to reflect your values: it's a short, memorable list (they only have three); it has tight language rather than more generic terms such as integrity or respect; it has behaviours that capture how they roll (and they can test employee candidates for these during interview); and they also employ an icon for each value so that they can be used in messaging, awards, and so on.

Dimple have brought theses values to life by publishing them on their website, they are reflected in the style of the benefits that they offer staff, and they are recognised in their quarterly Shine Awards.

These are great examples of companies who've really activated their values, but how far are they entrenched in the normal business psyche?

THE GROWING PROMINENCE OF VALUES

In a 2004 study conducted by Booz Allen Hamilton and the Aspen Institute,[2] a forum focused on values-based leadership and public

2 Chris Kelly, Paul Kocourek, Nancy McGaw and Judith Samuelson, *Deriving Value from Corporate Values* (USA: The Aspen Institute and Booz Allen Hamilton Inc, 2005). assets.aspeninstitute.org/content/uploads/files/content/docs/bsp/VALUE%2520SURVEY%2520FINAL.PDF

policy, senior executives from 365 businesses across thirty countries were questioned about their business's values.

The study found that not only were more businesses making their values available to the public than ever before, they were engaging in management improvement efforts driven by these values. These efforts included training their staff in values, appraising staff on their adherence to these values, and hiring business experts to address how values were impacting on their business's performance.

So why the current emphasis on values?

When values are alive in your business, your people know what is expected of them. They know what behaviour is required and what is unacceptable, and this gives them a framework for making independent decisions about how they work with each other and with your customers. 'Living' values also empower your people to cut superfluous activity and simply focus on what is in alignment with those values, a focus that will extend through all parts of the business.

One area where this is particularly relevant is when recruiting. Having clear values attracts the right staff, partners and customers, while filtering out the ones who aren't a match. Then, when every person agrees on the shared values of a business, they act as guidelines for their behaviour, making bureaucracy, rules and regulations largely unnecessary. In short, it takes the noise out.

Yet virtually no leader I meet can tell me what their business's values are. So, while there have been advances in preparing lists of values, I would argue that we're still a long way from a values-driven marketplace. Instead, most businesses either don't have values, or don't have values that *work*.

Those that don't have agreed core values will usually have unstated guiding principles that inform the behaviour of the business. However, without having created them consciously, they may be guiding their people in the wrong direction. For instance, a business that is driven by results may, either consciously or subconsciously, support cutting corners. While this may benefit the bottom dollar in the short term, it could lead to a deterioration of quality and performance that impacts safety, sustainability and profitability into the future.

Meanwhile, those businesses that *do* have values often don't live those values. Instead, they have assumed that because these values are written down, they will automatically become a part of the business, but this isn't the case in practice. The business doesn't hire people according to these values, staff don't act in alignment with these values, and management just puts up with behaviour that's out of alignment rather than cleaning it up. They are 'vapour values' that may have been espoused once and emblazoned on a plaque at the reception desk, but aren't reflected in the daily life of the business.

Enron, as most would recall, was a clear example of this in practice. In its Code of Ethics,[3] Enron listed the following values:

- 'Respect: We treat others as we would like to be treated ourselves. We do not tolerate abusive or disrespectful treatment. Ruthlessness, callousness and arrogance don't belong here.
- Integrity: We work with customers and prospects openly, honestly, and sincerely. When we say we will do something, we will do it; when we say we cannot or will not do something, then we won't do it.
- Communication: We have an obligation to communicate. Here, we take the time to talk with one another and to listen. We believe that information is meant to move and that information moves people.
- Excellence: We are satisfied with nothing less than the very best in everything we do. We will continue to raise the bar for

3 Enron Code of Ethics, Chairman Ken Lay's message to all staff. 1 July 2000.

everyone. The great fun here will be for all of us to discover just how good we can really be.'

The Code of Ethics went on to say, 'Enron stands on the foundation of its vision and values. Every employee is educated about the Company's vision and values and is expected to conduct business with other employees, partners, contractors, suppliers, vendors, and customers keeping in mind respect, integrity, communication, and excellence. Everything we do evolves from Enron's vision and values statements.'

Although Enron promoted these high-minded values, a widespread culture of fraud and deception existed at its upper echelons, and after the company's downfall many of its top executives were indicted or imprisoned.

Just writing values down doesn't make them happen.

Contrast that approach with Save the Children, a global not-for-profit dedicated to aid and development to help children, where I served as a Director on their Australian Board. There seemed to be rather more alignment between espoused values and values in use:

- 'Accountability: We take personal responsibility for using our resources efficiently, achieving measurable results, and being accountable to supporters, partners and, most of all, children.
- Ambition: We are demanding of ourselves and our colleagues, set high goals and are committed to improving the quality of everything we do for children.
- Collaboration: We respect and value each other, thrive on our diversity, and work with partners to leverage our global strength in making a difference for children.
- Creativity: We are open to new ideas, embrace change, and take disciplined risks to develop sustainable solutions for and with children.

- Integrity: We aspire to live to the highest standards of personal honesty and behaviour; we never compromise our reputation and always act in the best interests of children.'

The final issue is that while many organisations have values, those values aren't in alignment with their vision. This results in staff recognising the incongruence between the two, whether on a conscious or subconscious level. In a best-case scenario, employees who feel disconnected with the values will simply leave that organisation. In the worst-case scenario, the wrong people stay for the wrong reasons as, although they sense a disconnect, there are enough material benefits to retain them (and they probably see values-light businesses as the norm). Ultimately, they end up working on what they want to work on, in the way they want, rather than working towards a united vision. This laissez-faire approach has, unsurprisingly, mediocre outcomes.

While it may seem more obvious that a cause-related organisation will more easily frame and align with values, there is no reason for-profit organisations cannot do this well too.

LIVING VALUES IN PRACTICE

One of the defining experiences that led to my coaching career was my nine years at SMS Consulting, where I observed a highly successful business model that attracted and retained people whose personal values perfectly matched those of the company, which were 'add value', 'maintain unity' and 'enhance reputation'.

The difference with this company was apparent as soon as I embarked on the initial interview process for a role as a consultant. I'd heard that there was a very high fail rate at the interview stage, and I soon learnt why: SMS recruited a large percentage of high-performing, get-it-done types, but they also had to be the right 'fit' for the company's values. After an initial recruiter review, candidates were sent to meet potential peers, and an account/industry manager, before a final interview and offer with a senior leader. At any stage, a candidate could be eliminated if it was thought they wouldn't be a good fit. The result was a culture where most people got along, both at work and socially. What's more, SMS knew that designing a values-centric culture fostered greater commitment and better performance, but without the costly overhead of rules and bureaucracy that most businesses use to get alignment.

The non-bureaucratic environment of SMS meant staff enjoyed great freedoms, and it became clear to me that in previous organisations, the overarching workplace cultures I'd experienced had simply 'happened' rather than being by design, as it was at SMS. My realisation that a significant number of businesses lack the key, intangible asset of a belief system led me to explore how great businesses work – and ultimately, set up my own coaching practice to work with these types of businesses.

TESTING YOUR VALUES

If you are in a business that has values, the first test of whether or not they are 'living' values is simple. Pick a random member of your team and imagine sending them to a potential suitor looking to acquire your company or become a customer. What would that team member say about your business? What would they do? Based on their behaviour, do you think the acquirers or potential customers would understand the values of your business?

If your business has living values, they should be embodied by every member of your team. If some, or all, of your team members would fail this test, then your values aren't living.

A second, less theoretical, approach is simply to ask your team what they think your values are. Avoid anyone in marketing at first, as they are likely to be schooled in your business's PR messages. Likewise, those in upper management probably know what they are 'supposed' to say. Instead, go for the administration assistants, the client-facing staff and the back-office product people – those who are on the ground floor carrying out the grunt work of your business. What do they think your values are? What do they see demonstrated? Do they align with the values you want your business to embody? Then grab some of the newer staff members and ask them what the attractors were in working with you.

If you're like the majority of businesses I work with, you'll discover one of three things: your people aren't aware of the values you want them to uphold; there are fuzzy, albeit relatively aligned thoughts about the values; or they believe the business stands for different values to the ones you would choose.

In any of these cases, you need to bring values to the surface and communicate them for your business.

HOW TO DISCOVER YOUR BUSINESS'S CORE VALUES

The issue with most business's stated values is that they aren't 'living' values, they're aspirational. This typically happens because the HR department, PR or marketing teams come up with some values they think sound good to the outside world, rather than what is genuinely believed by the team. In short, they are the values that the business *wishes* it had. In my speaking engagements I tend to jest that someone likely Googled 'world's best values' and those are etched on a plaque that sits on the reception desk.

Interestingly, a business with living values doesn't require external justification. Instead, the values have intrinsic importance to those inside the business. For Bill Hewlett and David Packard at HP, respect for the individual was a deep personal value, not something they thought would make them look good for the media. Atlassian founders Mike Cannon-Brookes and Scott Farquhar are known for refusing to swap jeans for suits, which comes across in the down-to-earth language of their values. And in my experience at SMS, stringent hiring practices meant management were able to create a highly aligned workforce and culture.

You can't artificially create values and expect them to be authentic. You cannot simply make them up by looking at your competitors and others in the marketplace. Instead, values must come from within your business, and the process of creation is therefore one of discovery. Instead of making up core values, you need to discover and bring to the surface the values that already exist, and that you would like to guide your business.

So, rather than asking which core values you *should* have, think about the core values you *already* hold.

There are a number of approaches to discovering these values. The first is simply using your own top three values. If you are the founder, it's likely that your personal values have infused your business. The second is combining the common personal values across your team. Start by asking each person to list their five core values and, based on these lists, find the three to five that are the most common.

A third option, and the one I most commonly use with client leadership teams, is identifying several of your people who truly embody what you want your business to be. What is it about them that you want the business to emulate? What do they do that works? Can you condense those beliefs and behaviours into three to five core values?

The key to all of this is pushing relentlessly until you find your central values. If you end up with a list of more than five, you may be confusing your core values with operating practices. While operating practices may change, your values will be constant. In other words, if you asked the following questions about each value, you should be able to answer each one with a resounding 'yes':

- If your business entered a new industry, would you continue to uphold these values?
- Would you want your business to stand for these values for the next one hundred years?
- Would you want to hold on to these values, even if they became a competitive disadvantage?
- Would you fire those who breach these values consistently?
- Would you continue to hold these values even if you weren't rewarded for it?

Common examples of false values are elements like 'high-quality', 'consistency' and 'timeliness' – attributes you would like your product or service to attain, but which aren't necessarily values. The true test is whether you would still uphold those 'values' should they lose relevance in the marketplace. For example, if quality became irrelevant in your market in the next ten years, and the focus was instead on size or speed, would you still want to make that one of your core values? In most cases, the answer is 'no' – quality is a product attribute, not a guiding principle. And while it might be an element of your production strategy today, if things were to change tomorrow you would be willing to sacrifice it.

By contrast, 'acting with integrity' or 'providing excellent customer service' might be ideals that you would never sacrifice, regardless of external market forces. In other words, if the market didn't value these ideals, you would search for new markets that did. In this case, 'acting with integrity' and 'providing excellent customer service' *are* core values.

An important point to make here is that values are best phrased as verbs rather than nouns. Why? Because values guide the way your business behaves – the decisions you make, the processes you follow, the standards of your people – and verbs, which describe actions, are far more effective at guiding behaviour.

Let's consider the word 'innovation'. It's a common aspiration for many businesses today, but the word alone doesn't provide much guidance. How do you tell someone to be more innovative? How do you measure the level of innovation? If instead your value was based on a verb, such as 'always look at issues from different angles', this is far more valuable. When someone has fallen into a rut and you ask them to try looking at the issue in another way, this is far more concrete than telling them to value innovation.

PROPELLER TIP: For each value, draw out several behaviours that provide proof points that the value is being lived.

KEY POINTS

1. Values are fundamental business rules – in three to five clear, meaningful statements they capture the key immutable beliefs and behaviours of your business.
2. Many businesses do not have a clear, well-founded set of values. Others have aspirational values that are not 'living'. Either way, these are not a useful foundation in the belief system.
3. Clear values are critical as they represent the guidelines for what you should and shouldn't do. It's a collection of 'how we behave around here' statements.
4. Your values should serve as a foundation when making any important decisions, such as strategic choices, recruiting, and recognising and exiting staff.
5. To make your values endure and resonate, include them as a regular feature of corporate conversations and find ways to make them tangible.

TAKE ACTION

Do you know your values? Write them down now. Once you have a clear idea of your values, here are the questions you need to ask:

1. If you're the founder, owner or senior leader, how well correlated are your personal values and the company values?
2. Is there an underlying sense of values within your wider business group, or is everyone living by their own, rather than shared, beliefs? What counter-values behaviour have you noticed?

3. Would the team continue to hold these values even if they weren't rewarded for them?
4. How could the behaviours that underly your values be better described?
5. How could you do better at bringing your values to life? Do you base your offer, recruitment, recognition and strategy on them? Have you sacked team members for ongoing or significant values breaches?

CHAPTER 3

Vision

'In order to carry a positive action,
we must develop here a positive vision.'

Dalai Lama

A NOBLE QUEST

You now know your purpose, or *why* you do what you do, and have established values to guide the *way* you do it. The next step is clarifying *where* you are going. This destination, this vision, is the way you start to bring your purpose to life.

For example, if your *purpose* is to prove your physical potential, your *vision* might be becoming the greatest mountain climber in the world. If you are a doctor and your *purpose* is to heal, your *vision* might be to eliminate the need for human donors for people who suffer organ failure.

Do any of these statements resonate with you?

'Our vision is to be Earth's most customer-centric company; to build a place where people can come to find and discover anything they might want to buy online.'

> *'Empower every person and every organisation on the planet to achieve more.'*

> *'Our vision is a world in which every child attains the right to survival, protection, development and participation.'*

They belong to Amazon, Microsoft and Save the Children, respectively.

Your vision is the ultimate way in which your business can express its 'why'. However, it shouldn't be confused with a goal. A goal, no matter how big, can be broken down into milestones, which means it's attainable. A vision should stay just out of your reach, so you always have something to strive for. This is what keeps you and your business hungry. This is what keeps you and your business looking for new goals to manifest that vision. It's a noble quest rather than a specific destination.

In the mountain climbing example, where the purpose is to prove physical potential, the vision is to become the greatest climber in the world. Your goal might then be to climb Mount Everest. While climbing Everest is an enormous feat, it is ultimately achievable and measurable, so it is a goal rather than a vision. Becoming the greatest climber in the world, however, may always be unattainable, which will keep you focused on new ways you can work towards this vision once you reach Everest's summit.

Consider the doctor's purpose to heal, with the vision being to eliminate the need for human donors for people who suffer organ failure. The greater goal might be creating artificial organs. While that will contribute to the vision, it is unlikely that the need for human donors will be fully eliminated in a lifetime. So, where the goal could be attainable, the vision will always just be out of reach, which will lead to a new goal once the first has been achieved.

A business's vision must also be all encompassing. While individual departments or teams may have their own smaller goals, the entire business must be united by a single vision. This enables your staff, clients and partners to join the journey and embark on a common adventure. Once they are enrolled, they can then contribute to the big vision in their own way, leading to continued motivation for your staff, and your business extending its reach.

However, like purposes and values, this is another area with which businesses struggle.

WHY IS CREATING A VISION SO CHALLENGING?

Business leaders often have trouble creating exciting, empowering visions. Instead of choosing the dream, they try to analyse their way into the future. However, this approach is inherently limiting, as if you start by focusing on what you are capable of now, you are never going to be able to make big leaps.

Yet rather than rising to the occasion, many businesses just don't worry about the vision piece of the puzzle. Instead they just focus on running the business machine every day, comparing their performance to their annual budget, or last year's results. Or, like purpose and values, they use an 'off-the-shelf' vision. These visions are often concocted as a PR exercise to make the business look more appealing to outsiders. However, this results in shallow 'marketing-style' visions that don't have the authentic substance to become the driving force of a business. Because they aren't based on a business's beliefs, no-one believes them, so no-one works towards them.

Instead, the focus should be on creating a desired future, one that isn't over-analysed or off the shelf. Your task is not to predict what's possible or try to become what you think the market wants. Your only task is to choose a vision that feels inspiring, exciting and, most importantly, out of reach, and then do everything you can to move closer to it. *This* is what propels business performance – choosing your destination before figuring out how you are going to get there.

FINDING YOUR VISION

'Strategic planning is worthless –
unless there is first a strategic vision.'

John Naisbitt, futurist and author

Just like our mountain climber and doctor, your vision should start with your purpose. Take a moment to reflect on your *why*. Then ask yourself – what is the ultimate way you could bring that to life? How big could that be? If money was no object, if time was no object, what would you love your business to achieve to embody your purpose?

Richard Branson and Virgin embody their discovery-based purpose of being disruptive and 'changing business for good' by continually seeking out new challenges in new industries.

Businesses that have a purpose founded on excellence don't bother competing on price, because they can't uphold the ideal of excellence while selling commodities. Instead their focus is on continually outdoing themselves – creating something more beautiful, more refined, with better performance and of higher quality. The ultimate vision should focus on quality – if it is sacrificed for any other ideal, your business will lack congruence.

Altruistic businesses must have a vision that encompasses openness and integrity, leaving no room for hypocrisy. If an altruistic business is seen as sacrificing employee needs for the customer's benefit (or worse, the shareholder's benefit), they are not seen as walking the talk. Instead, altruistic businesses need to focus on the success of every group that touches the business, not just one or two. If this is you, your vision should encompass customers, staff and shareholders, rather than sacrificing one for another.

Meanwhile, heroic businesses have visions that focus on strength, competition and overcoming impossible obstacles. You want to focus on being the best – if you cannot strive to be the leader in your field, then you should choose a new field (or a new purpose). This is the reason Jack Welch mandated that General Electric had to be number one or number two in every industry in which it participated. If not, GE left that industry.

So, ask yourself again, what is the ultimate way your business could embody its purpose?

BRINGING YOUR VISION TO LIFE

Once you have an idea, the next step is to create a vibrant, engaging description of your vision. What would the world be like if you actually achieved it? What would it be like if your descendants achieved it?

In 1913, Henry Ford's vision was to democratise the automobile, and he wrote:[1]

> *'I will build a motor car for the great multitude. It will be large enough for the family but small enough for the individual to run and care for. It will be constructed of the best materials, by the best men to be hired, after the simplest designs that modern engineering can devise. But it will be so low in price that no man making a good salary will be unable to own one – and enjoy with his family the blessings of hours of pleasure in God's great open spaces.'*

The difference between this and other visions is that most have been tweaked and refined by department after department, manager after

1 Casey, Robert H. *The Model T* (Baltimore: Johns Hopkins University Press, 2008).

manager, PR person after PR person. And, in that tweaking and refining, they have lost something. They have lost the emotion, the passion and the conviction that made them so compelling (if it was ever there to begin with).

This is why your vision isn't simply a wordsmithing exercise. It is supposed to be from the heart. It is supposed to be emotive. It's only then that it will rouse people to support and launch your business into the next stage of its journey.

One approach to bringing your vision to life is taking some time with your leadership team to imagine what it would look like if your business achieved this unreachable, impossible vision. What would others say about your business? How would you describe the culture? What does it feel like to work there? Which publications would write about you?

Have each member of the team choose the publication they imagined and write the article that was published about your business. Once the articles have been written (they don't have to be perfect), share them with the group. Choose the three to five most exciting snippets from these articles and use these snippets to form a vivid description of your vision.

PROPELLER TIP: Imagine yourself in the future and write or talk about your business in the present tense. What are people saying about it?

FORGET ABOUT WHAT'S 'POSSIBLE'

Many businesses I encounter through my coaching work struggle with the vision exercise because they start with where they are now. They consider their size, their specialities, their customer base, the market conditions, their annual revenue and their growth to date. And they use these data points as the basis for extrapolating a vision.

If, however, you start with your vision, you can then work back from there. And this will force you to work harder, expand faster, and do more than you thought was possible *today* so you can move closer to your vision *tomorrow* ... just like Brian Scudamore.

Scudamore dramatically scaled his Canadian-based junk removal business 1-800-GOT-JUNK from $1m revenue in 1997 to a group revenue exceeding $300m within twenty years. The turning point, according to Scudamore, was to envision what he wanted the business to look and feel like within five years. In what he describes as his 'painted picture', Scudamore went into deep detail, including the quality of the trucks he would have, the number of franchises, getting profiled on the Oprah Winfrey show, the things his customers loved about working with them, and how his employees would describe the business to their families. He framed it and put it on the wall in the office, and within five years almost one hundred per cent of the vision had come true.[2]

These sorts of stories engage the mind and the spirit, so, ahead of the annual strategic planning sessions that I run for clients, one of the homework tasks is for the leadership team to spend time thinking about the future 'picture' of the business. It sets the scene for the strategising that we'll be doing. And let me just call out the elephant in the room for readers who are rolling their eyes at 'visualising the future'. There is a growing body of evidence on successful leaders pointing to vision as a key component of organisational outperformance.

So, let's return to the idea of your vision. What would be the ultimate expression of your purpose? What will your business look like in fifty years? What will it feel like for employees? What about

2 Scudamore, Brian, 'This Visualization Technique Helped Me Build a $100M Business', *Inc.*, 21 October 2015.

for customers? What is a publication that you would love to feature your business, and what will they say about you? Think of it as the ultimate form of storytelling.

And don't stress if you can't currently get your mind into the long-form version; a compelling vision can be captured with a single powerful sentence, such as those I highlighted at the start of the chapter.

When I first met my client Damien James, the founder of aged-care podiatry firm Dimple, his vision was one of the first things he talked about:

> *'Our vision is to change the way the world views and celebrates elders.'*

As I thought about the elders in my own family, I was inspired by Damien's vision and wanted to help him. It sets a challenge, makes us look beyond ourselves, and demands creativity of us at the same time. This is what we're after when we craft our vision – setting out an aspiration that people want to support. In that one simple sentence Damien conveyed a worthy vision that made a connection and touched an emotion.

Remember that the test of a vision doesn't come down to analysing whether or not it is possible. The test is whether it excites you. How do your people react? Does it spark ideas and spur momentum? Is it so compelling in its own right that you could go away for three months and your business would continue working towards it?

If so, you've built the foundations to spur your business into a new stage of growth.

KEY POINTS

1. Your vision is the ultimate way for your business to express its 'why'.
2. Few businesses build a vision that truly inspires and resonates with their team. Instead of choosing the dream, they try to analyse their way into the future.
3. The vision needs to be a 'what could be' rather than a 'what we are capable of' statement.
4. It speaks to a core ideal or emotion that engages the spirit of your business.
5. When developing a vision, don't start with today. Begin with your vision and work backwards and your strategy shows how you'll get there.

TAKE ACTION

Forget what's possible and don't think about today. What is your true vision? Now, answer these questions:

1. Does this vision excite and engage those who hear it?
2. How could you more vividly describe your vision?
3. What needs to be added to your vision to fully and authentically express your passion and emotion?
4. How well does your vision description conjure images of what life/business would be like once it was achieved? (Can you see yourself there?)
5. What else could be done to bring your vision to life?

PART II

Aspiration

'A noble man compares and estimates himself
by an idea which is higher than himself;
and a mean man, by one lower than himself.
The one produces aspiration; the other ambition,
which is the way in which a vulgar man aspires.'

Marcus Aurelius, Roman Emperor

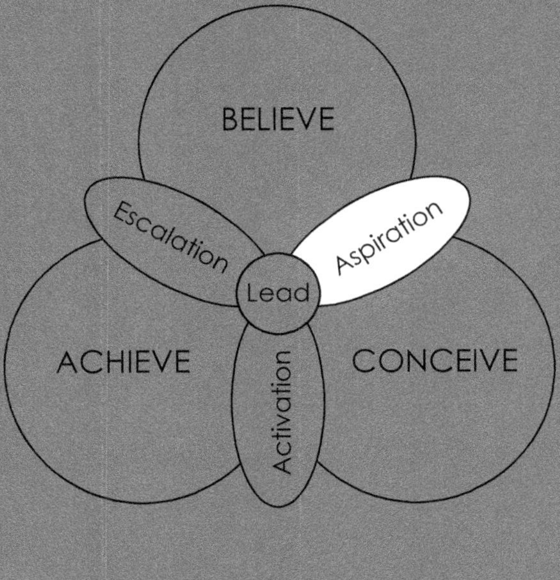

ASPIRATION is the propeller blade that connects the *Believe* stage to the *Conceive* stage. It's about making your purpose, values and vision concrete so that they can inform your strategy choices. And the best way I've found to do this is with what Jim Collins termed a BHAG … a big, hairy, audacious goal. Then we need to bring in consideration of the customers … what is *their* aspiration? Finally, we need to think about our organisational capability to deliver on these aspirations.

CHAPTER 4

The big, hairy, audacious goal

'The greatest danger for most of us
is not that our aim is too high and we miss it,
but that it is too low and we reach it.'

Michelangelo

THE EMBODIMENT OF YOUR BUSINESS'S PURPOSE AND VALUES

Visions are extremely powerful. They rally the troops, giving them something to work towards. As the embodiment of your business's purpose and values, they are a way of demonstrating that your business is about more than just providing superior returns for shareholders or above-average salaries for employees.

Yet all too often business leaders only give superficial consideration to what their company stands for, rather than embedding a vision into their business's DNA. If you spoke to those on the ground floor of your business, you might find that not only would they struggle to see how their roles and day-to-day tasks fit into the overall business vision, they would even struggle to see what the business as a whole is doing to achieve it.

The reason is your vision isn't concrete. Yes, your vision should be inspiring and elicit emotion. It should reflect the values and purpose of your business. But if that's all it does, it can quickly become disempowering as people struggle to bring that vision into their work. In the worst-case scenario, it will soon be forgotten as your team go back to doing things the way they always have.

The mistake I see most businesses making is they fail to connect their vision to their business strategies. And without being a part of the business strategy, there is no way your people can contribute to achieving it.

You want your vision to do more than inspire. You want it to *empower*. This is the advantage smart companies have – the unseen spiritual energy that comes from a strong, shared set of beliefs that drive aligned, positive action.

To achieve this, you can't simply tell your team the new vision and expect them to integrate it into their day-to-day work. You need to help by making it more concrete. Only then can your vision inform your business strategy.

The starting point is creating what business expert Jim Collins calls a 'big, hairy, audacious goal' (BHAG) in his book *Built to Last*.[1]

WHAT *IS* A BHAG?

> *'Sound strategy starts with having the right goal.'*
>
> Michael Porter, Professor, Harvard Business School

If your values express the rules you're going to play by, your purpose is the 'why' behind everything you do, and your vision is the ultimate expression of this 'why', your BHAG is a ten-to-fifteen-year milestone that will set you on the path to achieving that vision.

So, if we return to the mountain-climbing example from the previous chapter, the person's purpose was to prove their physical potential. The vision for doing that was to become the greatest

---

1 Jim Collins and Jerry I Porras, *Built to Last: Successful Habits of Visionary Companies* (New York: Harper Collins, 2002).

climber in the world. The BHAG might then be climbing the ten highest summits in the world in the next fifteen years.

Unlike your vision, which is enduring, your BHAG has a measurable outcome and a clear finish line so that your people can work together to achieve it. By having a specific end point, your BHAG creates precise requirements around the performance, resources and capabilities necessary to achieve it, as well as creating a clear image of what success will look like.

So is a BHAG 'just another goal', then? No – a BHAG is differentiated by its size, both in the sense of the extended timeframe required to achieve it and in the magnitude of what you aim to do.

You need to think long term

Rather than focusing on the next quarter or the next financial year, BHAGs focus on the next decade or so.

This long-term perspective has been one of the keys to success for high-performance businesses. While most floundering businesses work towards short-term gains and get caught up in the latest fad – whether that is mergers and acquisitions, restructures, bringing in a new leader, fixating on their latest product, entering a new market or investing in some new technology – high-performance businesses focus on whether these approaches fit into their long-term plans. If not, rather than getting caught up in the excitement, they stay focused on the steps that build momentum towards their ultimate goal – their BHAG.

This long-term perspective has several benefits:[2]

- Your investors/shareholders are committed to your business for the long term, which makes them better partners who believe in your business and products.

---

2 Maureen Kline, '4 Reasons to Focus on Long-Term Strategy,' *Inc.*, November 13, 2014. inc.com/maureen-kline/4-reasons-to-focus-on-long-term-strategy.html.

- Risk management across significant trend changes is more effective, as this cannot be seen on short-term horizons.
- The long-term investment in relationships with your staff, customers, suppliers and community then creates stronger relationships, unlike those with a short-term, transactional focus.

When communicated well, this perspective is shared by all who come into contact with the business, including shareholders, employees, suppliers, clients and the community. These businesses look to build long-term relationships with all of their stakeholders. They focus on delivering customer value over the long term, rather than making the quick sale. They build sustainable partnerships. And they strive to fulfil their people, so that they want to stay engaged and continue contributing to the journey. As a result, this long-term perspective creates loyalty with all stakeholders.

The only way to create this long-term perspective is to find a uniting goal, something that the business can work towards in service of its purpose and vision, and in alignment with its values. It must be, by definition, of a scale and timeframe that requires thinking, imagination and effort well beyond what could be marshalled today.

You need to make it BIG!

Beyond being a long-term goal, a BHAG should be so big, so hairy and so audacious that achieving it will force your business to push and work and grow harder and faster than it ever has before.

The first benefit of this is that the final achievement is far greater and far more inspiring. The second benefit is this creates a sense of urgency, as you start to think that the only way you'll achieve your BHAG is to get started *now*. The third benefit is that if your business can't achieve your BHAG today (which it shouldn't be able to ... because it's that big), this statement of ambition will force it to become one that *can* achieve the BHAG. It makes the business consciously pull itself up, rather than simply rolling along.

If you consider any business or any person who has achieved their BHAG, the common thread is they had to evolve to do so. Reflecting on the time and effort and resources which had to go into that achievement, it's easy to see the business that finished the journey was very different to the one that started it.

Take for instance the Australian company Red Balloon, founded by Naomi Simson with a $25,000 personal investment, with the vision of changing the way Australians gave gifts forever. They realised they needed some way of knowing when they'd got there, so, in 2004, Simson created the BHAG to reach ten per cent of the Australian population with Red Balloon's gifting experiences. Over the next decade the company grew to forty-six employees, formed Red Balloon Corporate for corporate incentives, and migrated their online infrastructure to cloud-based services to manage the volume of holiday-season web traffic. In late 2013, they delivered their two millionth experience, reaching their BHAG two years ahead of time.

Despite Red Balloon's humble beginnings, Simson's ability to formulate a long-range objective meant that the company never rested on its laurels and was constantly pushing itself beyond its comfort zone and evolving in order to achieve its BHAG. To keep the BHAG in their sights, they kept track of progress on a massive scoreboard in their office and implemented an iPhone app that made the score public too. This helped motivate the team in their daily activities to ensure customers and suppliers had a great experience using their service. Day upon day, week upon week, these efforts built momentum and a brand. While the first million experiences took seven years, the second million took only two years.

The ultimate result ...

The ultimate result of a daunting ten-to-fifteen-year goal is it forces your leadership team to think of the future from a visionary perspective, rather than getting fixated on your current strengths and capabilities and working backwards to what is achievable. By breaking out of the pattern of thinking small about what can be achieved now, the focus shifts to the future, and what needs to happen to bring that to life.

Ultimately, this is the catalyst that spurs faster growth and development. It prompts positive questions that form the foundation of your strategic considerations, such as, 'How can we do that?' and, 'What can we let go that is holding us back?'

This then more widely and deeply engages the team, which boosts alignment across your business and increases the speed with which you achieve results.

PROPELLER TIP: Consider your BHAG as a multiple of your main revenue driver; for instance, episodes of service.

HOW TO CREATE YOUR BHAG

Think about what you would love your business to achieve in the next ten to fifteen years. Building on the Vision work from the previous chapter, imagine you are being featured in a media story or were listening to your introduction before a TED talk. What would you want people to say about your business? How would they describe your success?

When doing this exercise, forget your existing people, budget and capabilities. Instead, think about what you would love to achieve if time, money and other resources were no object. You want to stretch beyond what is currently possible – ideally you should choose a BHAG that you are currently only sixty per cent capable of achieving. That is, something that is achievable in the long term, but will likely require significant changes within your business to improve your chance of success.

If you're struggling to put your vision into a single BHAG, there are four approaches that can help give some direction:

- reaching a certain target
- defeating a big enemy
- emulating a role model
- achieving an internal transformation.

A targeted BHAG could be quantitative, like it was for Red Balloon to reach ten per cent of the Australian population. To set a quantitative BHAG, start with your headline numbers – what would you like your business to be worth? Do you have a profit or turnover target? How many people do you want to employ? How many customers do you want to serve? What percentage of market share do you hope to achieve? When it comes to qualitative BHAGs, you might instead consider the level of prestige, success or industry dominance you would like to achieve.

A big-enemy BHAG is typically a David-versus-Goliath situation – you want to take on a big player in your industry. For example, Nike's 1960s mission was to 'Crush Adidas', while Honda's 1970s BHAG was '*Yamaha wo tsubusu!*' ('We will crush Yamaha!'). If you want your business to be number one in your industry, the competition fuelled by a big-enemy BHAG can be extremely compelling fuel.

Role-model BHAGs can be very effective for up-and-coming businesses that want to make their mark on their industries. They involve choosing a role model, usually another business, and emulating its traits and, ideally, its success. Anyone who wants to be 'the Apple of' their industry has a role-model BHAG. The trick is choosing a role model that is inspiring for your people – if the role model you choose is obscure or doesn't reach them on an emotional level, then this BHAG won't have the desired impact.

Meanwhile, a BHAG that focuses on internal transformation is different to the first three in that it has an internal rather than an external focus. While some of the benefits of this internal transformation might include increased sales, growth and success, these are not the focus. For this reason, internal-transformation BHAGs are typically best suited to established businesses that need internal change to remain competitive and healthy.

For instance, right now your business may have an industry focus, perhaps serving a sector such as healthcare or defence. An internal transformation BHAG may see you completely switch focus from an industry- to a capability-based model. You may be technology or process experts who can repurpose your organisation to appeal to a wider customer base on the strength of these capabilities.

For instance, in the case of my client who runs a substantial services business with 1200 staff and $60m turnover, they have a BHAG of reaching $500m revenue. We know that they can achieve this by maintaining their momentum of twenty per cent growth each year for the next twelve years. But it will likely involve a substantial technology transformation in areas such as robotics, rather than just extrapolating current staff numbers to 10,000.

So when you consider where you would like your business to be in ten to fifteen years' time, is your BHAG about reaching a certain target, defeating a big enemy, emulating a role model, or achieving an internal transformation?

PUTTING YOUR BHAG TO THE TEST

Do you know your BHAG now? Write it down and let's put it to the test. A BHAG is only effective if it:

1. gives your business a clear, concrete goal to work towards
2. generates passion and emotion in your people
3. motivates action.

The beauty of the BHAG is that it opens minds, allowing companies to look far beyond where they may have ever considered taking their business. I've seen this powerful goal-setting method work effectively for many of my clients.

One such client was Damien James, the founder of Dimple which, as I've mentioned earlier in the book, provides aged-care podiatry services. I was impressed by the vision Damien had for his company from the get-go. Despite having been told by others that his business idea just wouldn't work, he possessed a single-minded determination that he could change the way podiatry was delivered in the aged-care space. His BHAG became 'to positively touch the lives of one million elders'. It was a big, bold number that was well beyond their scale at the time, but as you'll recall from the discussion about Dimple in the Believe section, this was clearly aligned with their care-based values, their purpose and vision, and it has informed the strategic decisions they have made to drive action since.

What really resonates about this company is that Damien, CEO Nick Beckett and their team shine a light on the fact that elders living in aged-care facilities deserve respect and excellent care, which is summed up by their vision to 'change the way the world views and celebrates elders, one smile at a time'.

With a concrete BHAG that aligned with the company's vision, purpose and values, Dimple grew from an idea into Australia's largest aged-care podiatry provider, generating more than $11 million in revenue annually and employing more than sixty-five podiatrists.

How does your BHAG compare? If it's clear, people should immediately understand what the business is working towards. When you share this BHAG with your leadership team, do they immediately know what you're talking about, or do you need to explain yourself? If you find yourself going into detailed explanations, go back to the drawing board.

If it's a real goal, it should be measurable. So, in ten to fifteen years, will you know whether or not you've achieved your BHAG? Do you need to look at your measurement capabilities? Is the BHAG itself vague or fluffy? If so, go back and tighten it up.

In my own business, my BHAG is to help 5000 Australian businesses, which is ten per cent of the mid-tier market. It is a substantial goal, considering that I only work one-to-one with around a dozen businesses at a time, so it can't be done using my current business model. I'll need to pivot part of my business into one-to-many offerings (and some of you might already have worked out that my book is part of that strategy). So, it will take massive action and require persistence, passion and energy … but to me this is critical and inspiring work as the mid-tier market is the engine room of a vibrant, growing economy.

To generate passion and emotion in your people, the BHAG needs to be clearly connected with your business belief system. Will chasing this BHAG be congruent with your values? Is it delivering on your purpose? Finally, does your it present as a natural extension of your vision? Then, when you share your BHAG with the team, how do they react?

To create a sense of urgency and motivate action, it needs to be a stretch. Are you currently only sixty per cent capable of achieving your BHAG? Would achieving it in the next ten to fifteen years force your business to dramatically grow or improve its capability? It needs to at least be a misty image in the distance, where, although it's a stretch, your people can make out the shape of the future. If the image is too blurry, it will seem not even remotely possible, which will fail to galvanise the team. Indeed, it can have the reverse effect – they will think the leadership group are 'away with the fairies' and fail to engage.

Finally, consider carefully whether or not the BHAG is really achievable. Yes, you will need new people, new capabilities and new resources. You may need to invest at a greater level than you ever have before, restructure your business, and enrol the best people in the industry on your mission. But, if you were able to fully commit to doing everything necessary, could your business achieve this BHAG?

If so, we'll shortly be using it to inform your strategy.

KEY POINTS

1. A BHAG gives you a focus for the future scale and scope of your business – it puts a metric to your vision.
2. Despite its importance in driving growth, having a BHAG – or having one that works – is rare in the business community.
3. The BHAG is a substantial timestamp or milestone that defines your business success in ten to fifteen years' time. Unicorns aside, it is typically not achievable in the short term.
4. Your BHAG should be something that, right now, your business only has a sixty per cent chance of achieving. Make it BIG.
5. It should provide the clarity and emotional charge to engage the hearts and minds of the whole business and motivate action.

TAKE ACTION

Let's critically assess your BHAG. Do you already have a BHAG? If not, re-read this chapter and make a start, then answer these questions:

1. Is the BHAG sufficiently exciting (both for you and your staff)?
2. How clear and easy to understand is it?
3. In terms of congruence, how well does it connect with your values, purpose and vision?
4. Will it be a stretch in the right direction? Would it be remarkable if you achieved this?
5. In ten to fifteen years, how will you be able to tell if you've achieved it? Write this down.

CHAPTER 5

Customer

'The most important single thing is to focus obsessively on the customer. Our goal is to be earth's most customer-centric company.'

Jeff Bezos (Amazon founder)

Before you can take the next steps to achieve your BHAG, there is a key partner that you need to make sure is on board to have any chance of success: your customers. All too often I meet business leaders who have established their products and services, but as these have grown the company has become internally focused and allowed its customers' needs to become a secondary consideration. So, while it's very important to have a clear and motivating aspiration for your own business, you must equally ensure that you understand and align with the aspirations of your current (or future) customers.

UNDERSTANDING YOUR CUSTOMERS

There are three important lenses to look through when understanding your customers:

- Who is your 'core' customer?
- How can you best deliver to them to maximise your results?

- What is the customer experience they want?

Let's have a look at each of these.

Who is your 'core' customer?

In terms of the first lens, ask yourself some basic questions to gain a better understanding of your 'core customer', as marketing and brand expert Bob Bloom would call them.[1] That is, your principal customer base that most values what you do and generates the greatest financial benefit. Where are they, and what are they trying to achieve? What is the obstacle standing in their road that you can move? Taking this a step further, it's helpful to develop a detailed profile of a 'typical' core customer to better understand them and help you better direct your efforts to find and serve them. Consider the following:

- What is their gender (if applicable) and age?
- What is their role?
- If they are business owners, what is the size of their business?
- What are they fundamentally trying to get done?
- What are their wants and needs – is it price-based, turnaround time, service, product range?
- Do they have particular qualifications or professional/trade affiliations?
- What is their personal style?
- How do they like to engage with you? (For example, are they social or more arm's length?)
- What sort of outside interests do they have?
- What is their annual (or perhaps lifetime) value to your business?

1 Robert Bloom, *The Inside Advantage* (McGraw-Hill Education; 1st edition, 2007).

For instance, my typical client is a forty- to sixty-year-old type-A energetic business owner/CEO who is a humble leader, often a member of a business group like EO, YPO or TEC, is curious to learn and be challenged, as they seek to grow their established mid-tier business and boost its performance.

In your own business, if you only have a vague idea of who they are or you try to cast your net too widely, you'll struggle to tailor a winning strategy with a clear target. Having a clear idea of who your ideal customer is will let you tune in to their specific pain points and the gains they're seeking, help you tailor your products and services to them, and keep them at the front of your mind as you go on to shape your strategy. Going back to the Jeff Bezos quote at the start of the chapter, he has encouraged having an empty chair at every Amazon meeting as a reminder to his staff that they need to have the customer 'at the table' when they're making decisions.

PROPELLER TIP: Give these core customer personas a name so you can talk about them as a real person inside your business.

How can you best deliver to them to maximise your results?

The second lens relates to the demand for your product or service. By knowing the needs of your customers, you can optimise your business and weight your efforts towards fulfilling them. Could a likely source of profitability for your business be a customer whose needs have been ignored by your competitors?

In *How Companies Win*, authors Rick Kash and David Calhoun argue that in a world that is largely oversupplied, businesses need to segment their customers according to the nature of their demand.[2]

2 Rick Kash and David Calhoun, *How Companies Win* (New York: Harper Collins Publishers Inc, 2010).

For instance, they found a powerful distinction among dog owners. Rather than segmenting owners according to the type or size of their dog, which is the usual approach, they looked at the *role* of their dog. They found that a small but highly profitable niche of owners had their dogs as a sports-training companion, and were therefore prepared to feed them a tailored nutrition product. If a dog-food company catered to this niche, they would experience a marginal cost lift in delivering the product, but be rewarded with a substantial increase in profit.

So, thinking about your business and its customers:

- What are the different demands of your ideal customer? (Why do they want your product or service?)
- How does your current portfolio of products and services map against this demand?
- Which areas of demand are most profitable and, knowing what the customer is *really* trying to get done, which areas of latent demand could you tackle?
- What does the offering need to look like to serve these customers well?

What do they value most?

There's an exercise I use with my clients called the Attribute Map, which I learned from authors Anne Morriss and Frances Frei, that will help you visualise your customers' wants.[3] First, take a blank piece of paper and draw a graph with a vertical and horizontal axis. To the left of the vertical axis, list around five to ten attributes that they value the most (for instance, price, responsiveness, range of products/services, quality, personalised service) towards the top, descending to the least valued towards the bottom.

3 Frances Frei and Anne Morriss, *Uncommon Service* (Boston: Harvard Business Review Press, 2012).

Now think about how well your company performs when it comes to delivering each of these attributes to your customers. Using the horizontal axis to measure this, plot on the graph which attributes your company caters to well (towards the right) and which it caters to poorly (to the left).

The second part of the exercise is to plot where your main competitors sit when it comes to the same attributes. Once you've plotted this, you'll have clear picture of how well your business meets customer demand in comparison with your rivals. When you're done, go to your customers and ask them directly how they feel your company performs against each attribute, and how this stacks up against your competitors. This may be as formal as a questionnaire for a larger group of customers or as informal as catching up for coffee with some of your regular key clients.

PROPELLER TIP: Where is the 'white space' where you can be valuably different from your competitors?

Usefully, my clients typically find that their top three attributes become the succinct 'brand promise' for the business that represents how they'll want to stand out. For example, among my clients, a regional food manufacturer client identified key differentiators around provenance, authenticity and value as the top attributes that appealed to their core customers. Meanwhile, over at my client UCS Group, a specialty infrastructure services business, they landed on 'safe, on time, first time' as the three tenets of their brand promise. And to make it clear externally and hold themselves accountable, they've painted it onto their building (inside and out), their vehicles and embroidered it onto their workwear.

Gaining clarity around those attributes that your clients most value (and indeed those attributes they actually care about less) will be invaluable for informing the choices you will be making as you work through this book and shape your strategy and business model.

What is the customer experience they want?

The final lens, once you understand the relative importance of the attributes, is the overall customer experience. Business author Gary Hamel advocates an empathic thinking approach to evaluating this.[4] That is, considering what the emotional states of your customers are as they negotiate each step of their experience with you.

Ask yourself the following questions about your core customer:

- How do they first become aware of a need for your products and services?
- How do they learn more about, and compare, you and your competitors?
- What is the purchase process and experience like?
- How do they get access to or take delivery of your product or service?
- Having received your product or service, how do they find the in-use experience?
- What is the post-purchase experience for the customer?

One business whose success came from an understanding of customer need is the Australian-owned mergers and acquisitions (M&A) company Ansarada. Before starting the business, its founders were working in the same field and looking for a virtual data room to help manage their challenges. When they came up short, they decided to

4 Gary Hamel, *What Matters Now: How to Win in a World of Relentless Change, Ferocious Competition, and Unstoppable Innovation* (San Francisco: Jossey-Bass, 2012).

go out to market, find out what was most important to dealmakers like them, then make a product that was significantly and remarkably better than what already existed. Now Ansarada creates software to help make M&A transactions easy. Twelve years later, 10,000 deals have been completed thanks to Ansarada.

Ansarada's founders understand their clients because they too were customers, unable to find the right solution for their problem. Their customer-centric approach remains embedded in the company's promise to 'make life easier for our clients every day'.

* * *

So, in summary, the customer insight needs to be:

- Who are they?
- What do they value?
- What is their journey to get it?

By putting yourself in the shoes of your own customers and examining them through the three lenses we've explored, you'll be ready to turn your focus to the capability your business needs to meet customer demand.

KEY POINTS

1. Success will come from a strong focus on serving your most important customers.
2. Many businesses, though, become increasingly internally focused as they grow, to the detriment of the customer.
3. You must develop a clear idea of who your core customer is before you can understand their needs.
4. Core customers whose most important needs can be identified provide an opportunity for focus, differentiation and profitability.
5. It's essential to examine the thought process and emotional state your customers experience when they engage with your product or service so that you can better satisfy their needs.

TAKE ACTION

Does your business have a clear understanding of its customers and their needs? Ask yourself these questions:

1. Who is your target customer? Create a profile detailing their characteristics.
2. What are the needs of this customer? How would those attributes be ranked in importance from high to low from the customer's perspective?
3. What type of customer experience do they want?
4. Is there a segment of customers whose needs are not currently being met that you can tailor your product or service to meet?
5. Is there sufficient market size among these customers? Where are the trends taking demand?

CHAPTER 6

Competency

'Consistent alignment of capabilities and internal processes with the customer value proposition is the core of any strategy execution.'

Robert S. Kaplan, Professor, Harvard Business School

THE VALUE OF YOUR UNDERLYING COMPETENCIES

The likelihood of success in satisfying your customers' needs and achieving your own business objectives is directly correlated to the competencies your business currently has or is able to develop or acquire. Herein lies the challenge for many businesses: they typically see themselves as a collection of functions and processes that delivers a product or service rather than thinking about the underlying competencies. For a company such as Honda, one of their core competencies would be 'the design and production of small engines', which gets them into a breadth of markets such as lawn mowers, boats, motorcycles and pumps.

Gary Hamel and CK Prahalad describe these competencies as the root system of a business.[1] Separate to your specific products, services, functions and processes, they provide the sustenance and

1 C.K. Prahalad and Gary Hamel, 'The Core Competence of the Corporation', *Harvard Business Review*, May 1, 1990. hbr.org/1990/05/the-core-competence-of-the-corporation.

stability for what you do. Indeed, the power of a core competency lies in the fact that there is no single product, process or resource that captures it. Rather, it is the unique way that your business differentiates itself by combining all these aspects that makes it valuable to your customers and gives you access to attractive markets, while being difficult for your competitors to copy.

What are the underlying competencies in your own business? What are those collective learnings and skill sets that differentiate you from your competitors and are highly valued by your customers? Review the key steps in delivering a product or service to your customers and consider the following:

- What specific aspects of this approach brings customers to you? (What do they value?)
- What sits behind or supports you doing what you do? (This could include things like 'a world-leading design team' or 'brand positioning'.)
- What are the three to five things that separate you from your competitors? (You may get some clues from the previous exercises in the Customer chapter.)
- Of these, what are you really good at?

The benefit of this exercise is that once you have discovered your underlying competencies, you can leverage them for other products, services and markets. Take Uber, for instance, whose core competency has been to harness technological advances into convenient, easy-to-use and low-cost services for their customers. With its app-based transportation network now available in over fifty countries and 200 cities, Uber has leveraged itself into on-demand deliveries.[2] The

2 Cooper Smith, 'Inside Uber's Strategy to Become the Next On-demand Delivery Powerhouse', *Business Insider*, May 1, 2015. businessinsider.com/ubers-on-demand-delivery-ambitions-2015-4?IR=T.

company has a number of big-name brands using the on-demand delivery offer; its GPS-based software has been upgraded to enable multiple assignments; and Uber can consolidate all its services with this technology.

For another example, look at Atlassian's competency in staff engagement. It has many facets and therefore is not easy to duplicate or imitate:

- a strong set of core values that is alive in the organisation
- culture-focused recruitment
- an onboarding process that gets new hires contributing in week one
- a focus on team health and building high-performing teams
- a commitment to giving back to the community
- valuing individual strengths and work styles
- an agile culture that values innovation.

Unsurprisingly, they are regularly rated in the top ten 'Best Places to Work'.

What are you *not* good at?

The other key consideration is what are you *not* good at? What are the low- or no-competency areas of your business? Rather than seeking to develop these, the approach that will see your business achieve your goals more quickly is offloading them, either totally or by devising a better, faster, or cheaper alternative. One of my clients – an accounting firm – determined that a chunk of their routine accounting compliance work was non-differentiated, was costing them a lot of money and was not highly valued by clients. They decided to offshore the low-value work to a highly capable back-office operation in the Philippines. Following training, the operation started delivering high-quality output at a significantly lower price within ten days of starting. Today, this low-cost approach is effective and profitable, and the head-office team are able to redirect the time and budget they have saved towards their real differentiating competency, which is high-touch customer service and advice.

FINDING YOUR COMPETENCIES

So, now that we've identified the value of leveraging our competencies, how do we go about identifying them? There are a couple of things that I work on with my clients that help to draw this out:

1. Look back to the Customer chapter which teased out the most valued attributes of your offering and, in particular, the top attributes that reflect your brand promise. What are the learnings and skill sets that have enabled you to perform well here?
2. Every business, whether or not they have codified it, is sitting on a 'recipe' of principles and practices that taken as a bundle represent 'my business in a box'. Jim Collins and Morten Hansen refer to this as a SMaC Recipe – the Specific, Methodical and Consistent way that companies go about their business.[3] Again, look behind each of the recipe ingredients for the underlying competency.

PROPELLER TIP: Once you've worked out your competencies, investigate whether you can legally protect them to enhance your advantage.

---

3 Jim Collins and Morten Hansen, *Great by Choice* (Harper Business, 2011).

In the case of my client Techni Waterjet, they'd built an international reputation for their leadership in high-pressure water-jet cutting, which had a variety of industrial applications from automotive parts production through to food, glass and stone applications. While Techni manufactured complete water-jet cutting machines as a product range, we determined that their central competency was in designing the high-pressure pumps and cutting heads which sat at the heart of each machine. This insight changed the way that the founders and owners thought about their business from its historical product-based focus to an intellectual property focus, and accordingly informed their strategic choice to sell a majority share in their product business and retain the key intellectual property assets.

* * *

By carefully examining the competencies of your business, you can begin refining that set of underlying strengths that makes it successful and unique, invest in areas where it falls short, and pragmatically abandon areas that are likely to hold you back as you move towards achieving your objectives.

KEY POINTS

1. Understanding these foundational business competencies is crucial to success.
2. Most businesses tend to think in terms of products and services, not the core competencies that deliver them.
3. Refine your areas of strength and invest in developing competencies where the business falls short.
4. There may be areas of your business you can outsource or abandon if you don't have or can't develop the competency to successfully compete in that domain.
5. Once you have identified and developed key competencies, you can leverage them into other products, services and markets.

TAKE ACTION

Ask the following questions to determine the competencies your business currently has or needs to develop in order to grow:

1. What are the underlying competencies of your business?
2. Which of them best separate your business from your competitors?
3. What must you do to protect and enhance these competencies?
4. In which areas does your business fall short, and how can you begin to address this?
5. What things is your business unlikely to ever do well? Can you outsource or abandon these operations to save time and money and reduce risk?

PART III

Conceive

'Strategy is the craft of figuring out which purposes are both worth pursuing and capable of being accomplished.'

Richard Rumelt, organisational theorist

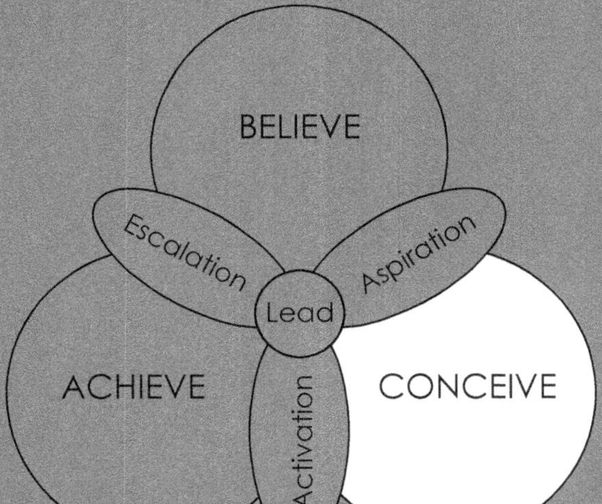

The **CONCEIVE** sphere focuses on crafting the strategy to achieve your vision and ultimately live your values and purpose through leveraging your competencies to address customers' needs. Accordingly, this part represents how you *think* about the business.

Businesses that are weak on this stage will drift. They have lower focus, and tend to behave reactively, only addressing the challenges that get thrown their way rather than working towards a thoughtful goal. These businesses are exposed to higher risk and can also become misaligned with customer needs. However, if you get this stage right, your business will have a clear roadmap to achieve your goals, align with your beliefs and deliver unique value to your customers.

CHAPTER 7

Strategy

'Strategy is about making choices, trade-offs;
it's about deliberately choosing to be different.'

Michael Porter, Professor, Harvard Business School

When I walk into a new client's office to kick off their strategic growth program, I often find they have at least a foundational sense of their beliefs and they are established at delivering their product or service, but something isn't working. They are frustrated and stuck; even after investing in more people, introducing new systems and developing their offering, their ambitions to grow and perform are not being met.

The invisible constraint is usually a lack of strategic thinking. It's like owning a powerful car yet not being able to engage the gears.

Your strategy is the roadmap that will take your business towards fulfilling your purpose, values, vision and BHAG, bringing your competencies to bear in serving your ideal customers' needs. Typically, your strategy will either be company-wide or focused on a specific business unit, and will include the actions you need to take, ideas you need to implement or policies you need to create, and the resources required to support each of these.

In other words, while your purpose was your *why* and your vision and BHAG were your *where*, your strategy is your *what*. In short: what choices you will make to deliver on your aspirations.

The major benefit of your strategy is that it makes your beliefs and aspirations tangible. Rather than just having another pie-in-the-sky dream, a strategically driven business is more credible and more capable of taking action. By contrast, businesses without a strong strategy typically espouse visions and goals but have no concrete way to achieve them, and their performance and credibility soon decline – they have no guiding direction.

A strategy clarifies the time, resources, money and capability required for you to achieve your objectives, which then gives you the ability to appropriately marshal and direct the resources necessary. This part of the approach also gives you the opportunity for a reality check on the goal you have chosen, helping you to determine whether or not you really want to achieve your lofty ambitions (that is, whether or not the investment would be worth the ultimate payoff), or whether a smaller goal would be more suitable for your business.

However, despite the importance of strategy, the majority of company strategies don't work. According to Robert S. Kaplan and David Norton in their article 'The Office of Strategy Management' – which took data from a study by Bain Consulting on 1854 large corporations – seven out of eight companies failed to achieve profitable growth, though more than ninety per cent had strategic plans with higher targets.[1]

Why this gap?

---

1 Robert S. Kaplan and David P. Norton, 'The Office of Strategy Management', *Harvard Business Review*, October 1, 2005. hbr.org/2005/10/the-office-of-strategy-management.

THE THREE MOST COMMON STRATEGY MISTAKES

While businesses make countless strategic mistakes every day, I've found these tend to fall into three main categories.

Category 1: Confusion between strategy and goal setting

Sometimes when a financial target is defined, businesses assume that garnering 'X per cent market share' or 'X million in revenue' is the strategy. They then expect that, if everyone understands the goal and there is enough support throughout the business, it will – somehow – be achieved.

However, confusing strategy and goal setting in this way fails to provide a roadmap for how to implement change. There is effectively a dream, rather than a structured set of ideas or capability developments to take the business from now to the desired future. While senior management asks their teams why they aren't hitting ambitious targets, the teams are left wondering *how* they are supposed to hit these targets.

In some cases, middle management will try to fill the strategic void by developing initiatives they think will help the business achieve its objectives. The issue with this approach is that these initiatives are typically uncoordinated at best and damaging at worst, resulting in confusion and finger pointing, and wasted time, money and resources.

For a strategy to be effective, it should focus on the actions, ideas, policies and resources required to achieve the goal, not simply the goal itself. This includes how the goal will be achieved, by whom, and by when. Without these details, the strategy is only an intellectual exercise without a business benefit.

I once assisted an American consumer products business where a new CEO had been appointed to address its stagnant regional revenue. The head office gave him a substantially elevated revenue number he was required to hit during his three-year tenure. His job was to work out how.

Fortunately, the CEO recognised the gap and engaged us to lead their team in crafting the required strategy. This included building relationships with fast-food outlets that leveraged my client's big-brand logos on their 'gift with purchase' offers. Another strategic plank was developing a program of family-oriented stage shows around globally recognised character brands. This was an active strategy around the world, so we built a challenging yet workable roadmap with defined steps for the regional team against which they successfully executed.

Similarly, your business needs a detailed strategy that maps out the path to meeting your goals.

Category 2: Refusing to let anything go

Unfortunately, a common mistake I see as a business coach is a business with a desire to achieve a goal by doing *everything* they are already doing.

For example, companies offering white-labelled products and services often have a choice between focusing on their wholesale business and focusing on branded strategies. However, many keep trying to play in both fields – on the branded side they might work on their customer packaging, online presence and customer service, while on the wholesale side they may focus on creating a new partner relationship team or looking for new white-label partners.

While all of these might sound like positive initiatives individually, they may not contribute to reaching your most important goal. The risk is that without an aligned set of objectives, which means letting go of non-aligned initiatives, it's difficult to build winning momentum.

In the case of one of my clients, a review of their product portfolio revealed that they had 200 products in their range … and yet seventy-five per cent of the profit came from just eight of those, while many of the unprofitable products were going to unprofitable, non-core customers. With hard data like this you have the raw material for leaders to make better decisions. In my client's case, it meant stopping the idea of building a big new factory – that wasn't necessary once they recognised the scale of their unprofitable products.

Businesses that become great are completely focused. They find one concept – or at least a small set of related, coherent concepts – and stick with it. This clarity defines what stays and what goes, as well as freeing up more resources to focus on the essential activities so they can achieve their goals more quickly.

Is your business trying to do too much at once? If so, what are you going to *stop* doing? Things like pet projects, misaligned or ego-driven acquisitions, and ineffective or unprofitable product lines need to go. It's particularly effective in sending a message to the wider organisation if you kill a sacred cow in the process. Lead by example and shut down one of your own pet projects that doesn't fit with your bigger goals (you know you've got one).

Category 3: Not focusing on customer value

The final mistake I see is that in the excitement of creating new strategies, some businesses don't consider whether these provide customer value.

In this case, businesses become more internally fixated on a product or service initiative than fulfilling customer needs. This usually results in businesses taking their customers for granted, assuming that they will want to buy, and continue to buy, whatever the business puts in front of them.

This rarely ends well. Your business's job is to provide value to your customers, and if you aren't fulfilling your brand promise, over time it's going to become more difficult to make a sale, let alone a profit.

One of the objections raised by some businesses at this point is, 'What if the customer doesn't know what they want?' Here businesses argue that their insight into their market has led them to conclude that the customer will want something that doesn't exist yet. This is the world of the disruptor – an inhabitable realm if you are willing to step up.

Consider Henry Ford, for example. He said that if he had listened to what the market wanted, they all would have asked for a faster horse. Yet the Ford Motor Company went on to become one of the world's largest and most profitable companies.

By contrast, when Coca-Cola launched New Coke in the mid-1980s, its reception was overwhelmingly negative. According to Richard Laermer, CEO of RLM Public Relations and author of *2011: Trendspotting for the Next Decade*, 'The tacky way it was introduced made it seem as though the regular Coke drinkers mattered little to the company and a boycott was started.'[2]

What was the difference? Why did one innovation fly while the other flopped? Put simply, Coca-Cola placed its product ahead of its customers, believing that innovation for innovation's sake would attract new customers. In actuality, it wasn't clear how New Coke provided any more value, tackled a pain or provided a gain for their customers. Henry Ford, on the other hand, was able to disrupt the market by thinking of his customers' desires first, before tailoring a more effective and efficient product that satisfied the basic need that existed.

2 Richard Laermer, *2011: Trendspotting for the Next Decade* (New York: McGraw-Hill, 2008).

No matter how detailed or inspiring your strategy is, if you can't bring your customers on board with your business, it's destined to falter. When formulating your strategy, use the customer profile and Attribute Map you created in part II of this book to consider whether you are providing them with true value.

HOW DO YOU GET YOUR STRATEGY RIGHT?

A bad strategy has wide-reaching consequences throughout a business, resulting in squandered resources, a deteriorating culture, the loss of top performers and a blunted competitive edge.

So how do you get your strategy right? Having established earlier in this book what it is your business does well, where it wants to go and what your customers want, you now need to closely consider three important questions:

1. Where is your business now?
2. What must be done to fulfil your bigger aspirations?
3. What will you stop doing?

Where are you now?

In 1993, IBM was in decline. That year the company experienced an US$8 billion loss and its share price was close to a quarter of what it had been six years prior. IBM's prospects were so bleak that Larry Ellison, the CEO of rival computer company Oracle, said, 'We don't even think about those guys anymore. They're not dead, but they're irrelevant.'

This was a time when the computer industry was fragmenting. Rather than companies offering complete, integrated solutions as IBM had done, separate firms provided chips, memory, hard disks, keyboards, software, monitors, operating systems and more. So IBM made plans to break up into smaller, more specialised businesses.

Enter Lou Gerstner. As the new CEO, Gerstner argued that in an increasingly fragmented industry, IBM's point of difference was being the only company that had expertise in all areas. In his book *Who Says Elephants Can't Dance?*, Gerstner wrote, 'At the end of the day, in every industry, there's an integrator', and he felt that IBM's brand, size and reach positioned it well to fill that role.

He argued that IBM needed to become more integrated, but by focusing on customer solutions rather than hardware platforms. In other words, rather than focusing on systems engineering, its primary activity would become IT consulting.

Nine years later, at the end of Gerstner's tenure, rather than making a loss of US$8 billion, IBM made a US$8 billion profit. The reason behind this turnaround was that Gerstner had completed a thorough evaluation of the situation – IBM's strengths and weaknesses, as well as the opportunities present in the industry – and crafted a strategy accordingly. In other words, Gerstner evaluated where IBM was at the time he stepped in as CEO, and used this information as the basis for his plan of attack.

What's in the way?

We've already collected some valuable inputs for our strategic considerations: what our belief system will let us do; what the customers expect of us; what core competencies we have; and the BHAG we're chasing.

As you've gone through those considerations earlier in the book you've probably started to form a view of 'where we are now' as a business. It's now time to bring those thoughts together as a current state assessment. Understanding your business's current state then feeds into the strategic choices you'll make and the actions required to deliver on them.

There are a couple of ways that I get my clients and attendees at my public events to come to grips with their current state. The simplest is just asking, 'What's in the way?' I often couch it in terms of, say, doubling their business. What is stopping them doing that right now? It typically yields useful insights into the state of the team, the health of their systems and processes, the quality and profitability of their products or services, and their customer cohort. We list them all, and usually end up grouping clusters of common elements that represent life as it is right now in the organisation (and it also serves to make some usually invisible disablers of the business more clear to the leadership team).

The Attribute Map, which we covered in the Customer chapter, also yields valuable information about what's going on right now. Seeing how well you're currently serving your clients' most important requirements is interesting (ideally strong performers on attributes they highly value, while happily weak on things they don't value). The story gets much richer, though, if you've taken the time to map the relative performance of your competitors. This will give you an insight into the competitive landscape and where the differentiation opportunities might lie. Are your competitors stronger than you on key attributes, or is this already an advantage you hold? Perhaps you are equivalent performers with your competitors and need to either find a way to be better or select a different customer niche or different basis for competition.

How do we make money?

Next, its useful to answer the question, 'How do we make money?' Given your competencies and customer expectations, what is the recipe within the business for serving up your wares? There are a couple of ways to draw this out: a popular one with my clients is the SMaC Recipe (which I referred to in the Competency chapter), whereby I ask them to draw out the ten to twelve specific, methodical and consistent principles and practices that underpin the operational performance of their business.[3] These typically relate to defining the core customer, the geographic area they serve, the product or service set, their staffing model, and so on. In short, if you had to hand over a brief instruction manual for your business, what would be in it? A more detailed approach is to formulate what Michael Porter called an Activity Map.[4] Here, with the fundamental customer value proposition or brand promise at the centre of the page, we map out all the activities (and the interconnections between them) that are carried out in service of the value proposition.

Each of these exercises gives us a richer sense of how the business works *now*. Importantly, this homework gives us an insight into what areas may need to be changed or built as we craft our strategy, the risks and exposures in our current model, and also the implications for communicating this during the Activation stage.

What are the trends?

Finally, beyond thinking about their own business challenges and the market, I also like clients to think about the wider world: what are the trends? These could be social trends such as higher density living, demographic trends including the transition of the baby boomer population to retirement, or technology trends such as the increasing role of artificial intelligence and virtual reality. What are we seeing competitors doing, and what is going on in adjacent industries that could affect our industry? For instance, I have healthcare clients that are considering how wearable devices that first emerged in the fitness industry could be used in service delivery.

---

3 Jim Collins and Morten Hansen, *Great by Choice* (Harper Business, 2011).

4 Michael Porter, 'What is strategy?', *Harvard Business Review*, 1996.

The point is we need to understand as a business where we stand with regard to the trends that are going on around us that will impact our business over at least the next three years for the current strategy and ten to fifteen years for the BHAG you've chosen.

Of course, we need to accept that none of this analysis is static. Some of the things you've captured in this exercise will be subject to changing trends, others impacted by competitor challenges, while others will be amenable to you driving your own changes.

For now, this analysis will set the context for implementing a comprehensive strategy to achieve your ultimate goal. Over time, though, you'll also want to develop a method of tracking trend changes, especially on those critical elements that have informed your strategy. You'll then be able to take thoughtful action as the field of play changes.

BREAKING IT DOWN

If we see the BHAG as a ten-to-fifteen-year goal, then deciding on the medium-term strategies is the first tranche of work that must be done to get us there.

Medium-term strategies: three to five years

For some businesses, this will be a relatively obvious and incremental advance on their current state. There may, for instance, be a natural geographic expansion, taking their offering into a new state or country. Perhaps there is a logical product extension that will happen after a current model is superseded. So it's a staged journey along the path they're already on. They'll remain similar to how they are now, just bigger and perhaps a little broader. A retail client of mine took this approach. They had a proven model for store rollouts and saw this as a revenue multiplier, so they plotted a logical progression into selected international markets.

The second approach, which I learned from my friend and colleague Kaihan Krippendorff, author of *Outthink the Competition*[5], is to project the likely trends in your industry over the next three to five years and consider how your business would fare if it continued to do exactly what it does now. While this may give you a somewhat uncomfortable view of the future, it will force you to consider what strategic changes need to happen within that timeframe if your business is to thrive. In particular, ask yourself the following questions:

- What would our preferred future look like? (Drawn from your vision.)
- What roadblocks are in the way that need to be overcome? (What's in the way?)
- Where is the emerging gap in the market that no-one is serving? (From your work on understanding the customer.)
- Is there something that looks really difficult, but could be highly effective and profitable if we can work out how to make it happen?

This exercise can help you devise a medium-term strategy you may not have previously considered and deliver your business to fertile new areas. The distinction here is that, instead of simply rolling your current state forward as proposed in the first approach, you stand yourselves at the end point and look backwards, asking: 'What must be done to get here?'

A third approach is to ask: 'Forget our own capabilities and what we are doing now – if we were coming in fresh to compete in this

---

5 Kaihan Krippendorff, *Outthink the Competition* (Wiley, 2011).

market, looking at what customers expect and the important trends, what would we do?' I tend to throw this question into my client team discussions to make sure they are thinking broadly enough – not only for their own business, but to be certain they've properly thought about potential competition from their current rivals or potential new entrants. For example, faced with this context, what would Uber do?

Through using one or a combination of these tools you should be able to generate numerous strategic options for the next three to five years. Then it's a case of testing them back against the work you've already done in this book. Based on your business's values and purpose, are there any strategies that you can't pursue? Which ones best leverage your core competencies? What choices will best deliver on the highest needs of your customers?

The goal is to generate up to five top priorities that best mark your way forward, along with success measures against them so you'll know if they've been achieved. They answer the 'what must we do?' question and become the strategic themes against which the annual plan and subsequent quarterly priorities will be set.

Over at my clients Ecotech, they derived their multi-year strategic pillars around 5Ps:

- *People* – engage, enable and energise our people to reach their full potential
- *Product* – create customer solutions that help shape their future
- *Partner* – actively seek partners who help us shape the future and serve our customers better
- *Presence* – offer our customers better service wherever they are
- *Process* – simple and efficient is good for us and great for our customers

Obviously these just capture the highest level essence and there is more detail internally around the specifics, but you get a sense of the intent behind these and how they aid clarity and communication.

PROPELLER TIP: Find one multi-year priority that could be a substantial multiplier of your business.

Short-term strategies: one year

With all this foundational work done, you're in a strong position to break down your medium-term strategies into one-year strategies.

A great way to think about this is by defining the performance cadence that you'll use to deliver your goals. Jim Collins and Morten Hansen refer to this as the '20 Mile March'.[6] The guts of this is to decide a pace or set of achievements that, no matter what, you're committed to attaining (that is, sunshine, hail or wind, we'll march twenty miles each day). It's a way of breaking down the BHAG and multi-year goals or capability developments into a doable rhythm. You can then test your choices for the year and ask: are these the necessary and sufficient initiatives to get us there?

In the case of one of my clients, a small and growing professional services firm, they decided on a cadence of $500k revenue increase each year. When we did the annual planning there was a much more focused session around the sales strategy as their current client base and business development approach was unlikely to yield the required $500k of growth. Accordingly, they refined their target market towards a top twenty-five cohort of larger prospects and developed a sales approach that would get them to the goal.

Another client has agreed to a 'twenty per cent march', committing to growing their business by twenty per cent each year. The

6 Jim Collins and Morten Hansen, *Great by Choice* (Harper Business, 2011).

reality check was that they had already experienced twenty per cent growth – the challenge was keeping that rate up as the numbers got bigger. When I ran the numbers, it means they would achieve their BHAG of $500m revenue in twelve years. So the cadence has both short-term and long-term relevance and relatability for them: what they're doing this year is readily connected with the bigger plan.

Given your ambitions for the medium term, what must be done towards each of those priorities in the current year? Considering this is important for two reasons: first, if you've picked the right goals, you should be doing some work towards them sooner rather than later. Second, it forms an important part of the alignment that you're developing within the business so that your staff can see how the tasks and timeframes relate to each other.

For example, one of my Melbourne-based clients has a three-year strategic goal of having offices in Sydney, Brisbane and Canberra, which will help them serve their national clients. Their one-year strategic goal is to gain a foothold in Brisbane, and one of their actions to get there is committing one to two days per week of sales effort in that city.

I encourage clients to develop a comprehensive list of all the things they think could or should be done during the year so there are plenty of options to consider. Then, as you did for the medium-term strategies, just pick the most important handful of things. What will make the biggest difference? What are the must-do tasks? And again, how will you measure their success? Ideally, you'll also agree a 'critical number' to be achieved; perhaps it's a required level of revenue, or number of products installed, or customers under contract. What will be the main barometer of success for your year? Will the strategic choices you've prioritised get you to that number? It's really useful to develop tension between the metrics and priorities – it keeps the game honest for your team.

WHAT WILL YOU STOP DOING?

Following the above steps, you have probably committed your business to carrying out a selection of new activities and investing in a range of new resources to achieve your multi-year and annual goals.

The next question is: which of your existing activities will you stop in order to direct more time and resources to this strategy? Are there certain products or services you will stop offering? Will you stop serving a certain niche market or group of non-profitable or non-strategic customers? Will a marketing strategy or a strategic partnership be put on hold? Remember that making strategic choices involves deciding both what you will do and what you *won't* do.

For a couple of my clients this has involved decisions to stop selling certain product lines, for another it involved deferring plans for expansion into the USA, while for another it meant a business model switch from being product-centric to IP-centric.

As I mentioned earlier, many businesses make the mistake of not letting anything go. They assume that they'll continue doing all their existing activities to the same standard while implementing a new strategy. However, unless you can readily increase the size or productivity of your team, your existing people are going to quickly become overworked (and the dollars will be over-stretched too). This will result in frustrated, unfulfilled employees, and customers who are receiving lower levels of service as standards start to drop. More insidious, though, is that the increasing clutter of activities works against the clarity and focus that you need for strategic success. Having the strength to say 'no' builds clarity.

So the question is not, 'Should I give anything up?', but rather, 'What must I give up?'

When choosing what not to do, it's not just about cutting out loss-making or under-performing areas. Like everything, it must come back to your purpose, values and vision. What is your business currently doing that isn't in alignment with your newfound purpose? Are there any processes and behaviours that aren't a match for your new values? Are there any activities that won't contribute to achieving your vision and strategic direction? These are the activities that should go. Keep in mind, it doesn't have to be a 'dump and run' exercise; the business or product that no longer suits you may find a new home within some other business, and you can apply the proceeds to your new way forward. The end result is that resources are freed up and can be diverted to your new strategy, and a powerful message about strategic direction and intent has been sent to your team.

PUTTING IT ALL TOGETHER

As you go through these steps, you'll discover the more people you involve throughout the business, the longer your strategy document gets. Too much detail makes communicating the strategy to the business difficult, as most people simply don't need to know the details that don't directly relate to them.

This is why I recommend capturing the key points that we've covered so far into a one-page strategic plan. Verne Harnish, author of *Scaling Up*, has developed a useful One Page Strategic Plan template that you can access and print from my web page. This will allow you to distil your overarching strategies and goals in a digestible format, and to consider how they align with your beliefs, purpose and values. It also forces you to decide the key actions and initiatives you will undertake – and how you will measure their success – to get your business to where it wants to go.

Once you've done this, you'll be ready to make the final preparations before you activate your strategies and bring them to life.

KEY POINTS

1. Your strategy is the essential roadmap that will take your business towards fulfilling its purpose and vision, living its values, and delivering on its BHAG.
2. A strategy clarifies the differentiating choices you make in serving your core customer and the time, resources, money and capability required for you to deliver them.
3. Businesses typically struggle with strategy because they don't really know what it is, they refuse to let anything go, and they don't focus sufficiently on their customers.
4. Your strategy must answer the question of how you can meet the expectations of and promises to your customers through the competencies that you either have or can get, while working within the bounds of your organisational belief system.
5. Framing your strategy comes from clarity regarding your current situation, insights into your core competencies and customers, understanding key trends impacting you, and the distinctive choices you then make to take the business forward.

TAKE ACTION

Consider what strategy your business will require moving forward and reflect on these questions:

1. Evaluate your current position. Where are you now? What would your ideal business look like and what is in the way of that at present?

2. What underlying trends could either help you surf or make you sink?
3. What is a real break-out opportunity that could significantly grow your business?
4. What must you stop doing to divert more resources to your strategy?
5. What must you do as a leader to make sure all strategic choices are clear and line up with your belief system, competencies, customer requirements and BHAG?

CHAPTER 8

Business model

'The same products, services or technologies can fail or succeed depending on the business model you choose.'

Alexander Osterwalder, business theorist

AN INSPIRED, CLEARLY DEFINED BUSINESS MODEL

In a world where retail clothing businesses have been under massive pressure, especially due to the growth of online business models, Zara has bucked the trend. With increasing sales, the brand was valued at more than $11 billion in 2017, with more than 2200 stores in ninety-three countries. How did they do it? Through an inspired, differentiated business model.

Zara has strategically set itself apart from competitors by sourcing currently trending fashion rather than predicting future taste (which decreases the risk of over-stocks and associated mark-downs), and by stocking small quantities and updating their stock twice a week, versus the competitor model of restocking once a season. This has seen the chain attract and retain a cohort of loyal customers who shop with a 'buy it while I see it' attitude.

Zara's success is just one example of the benefit of an inspired, clearly defined business model that sets a company apart from competitors. Yet most business leaders I encounter struggle to describe their model beyond, 'We sell product X to our customers'. Clearly, a business model is a little more complex than that.

NINE AREAS TO SHAPE YOUR BUSINESS

A key resource I often use with clients – Alexander Osterwalder and Yves Pigneur's Business Model Canvas (available at: businessmodel generation.com/canvas/bmc) – outlines what they call the 'nine basic building blocks that show the logic of how a company intends to make money'.[1] By gaining clarity on these nine areas, you will not only have a greater insight into how your business functions, but also *how* you can make changes to achieve your strategic objectives.

The nine areas that I get clients to consider in shaping their business model are:

1. *Customer segments:* Customers are the lifeblood of a business, and to serve them well you must understand their needs and desires. As discussed earlier in part II, make sure you understand who your customer is and what they want. If you serve multiple segments, be sure to know who your most important customer is.
2. *Value proposition:* Your value proposition is why your customers choose you over your competitors. What value do you deliver that they can't find elsewhere? Which of their problems do you solve? Which needs do your products and services satisfy?
3. *Channels:* Your channels are how you communicate with, distribute to and sell to your customers. Channels are relevant at all stages of the customer journey, from raising awareness about

---

1 Alexander Osterwalder and Yves Pigneur, *Business Model Generation: A Handbook for Visionaries, Game Changers, and Challengers* (New Jersey: John Wiley & Sons, 2010).

your products and services to providing after-sales support. How do you currently reach your customers? Which channels work best? Which of these are the most cost-effective?

4. *Customer relationships:* From personal assistance to automated service, every business has a relationship with its customers. What type of relationship do you have? Which relationships do they expect you to establish and maintain with them? How effective and how costly are these relationships?
5. *Revenue streams:* If your customers are your business's lifeblood, revenue is its oxygen. Think about the value for which your customers are willing to pay. What are they currently paying for? How do they pay, and how would they prefer to pay? How much does each revenue stream contribute to overall revenues?
6. *Key resources:* Resources are the critical assets that allow you to create and offer your value proposition, reach markets, maintain relationships and earn revenue. As a result, the nature and importance of the resources you need will depend on the business model that is chosen. What internal and external resources do you require to make your model work? Think about the human, financial, physical and intellectual assets you need.
7. *Key activities:* Key activities are the actions you must take to create and offer your value proposition, reach markets, maintain relationships and earn revenue. What is the chain of activities that deliver your end-to-end value proposition? For instance, in a product-based business, this might involve production activities, such as design, manufacture and distribution.
8. *Key partners:* Your business partners can help you offer your value proposition, reach markets and earn revenue. They can also help you reduce risk, acquire resources and carry out more key activities. So who are your key partners and suppliers?

How do they contribute to your key resources and key activities? What's in it for them?

9. *Cost structure:* What are the most important costs incurred to operate your business? Which key resources and activities are the most expensive? Is your business more cost driven (leanest cost structure, low-price value proposition, maximum automation, extensive outsourcing) or value driven (focused on value creation, premium value proposition)?

With these nine areas in mind, take some time to reflect on where your business is now. What is the current state of each of these areas? Does the combination enable you to effectively deliver your value proposition? Is it strong, sustainable and aligned?

There are two other important considerations now that you've built a picture of your current business model. First, what do the business models look like for your closest competitors? When you line them up side by side with yours, what do you notice? Perhaps they have a different channel to market, maybe their cost structure is advantaged in some way, or their value proposition might be solving a different slice of the customer problem set to yours. All things worth knowing, especially if you can draw an insight about the effectiveness of their overall model and how the pieces work together.

WHERE DO YOU WANT TO GO?

The second task, now that you understand how your own and your competitors' models work, is to design a go-forward business model that captures 'how' you will deliver on your strategy. Now that you've considered the various aspects of your business model, reflect again on strategy, aspirations and beliefs. Where do you want to go, and what do you need to do to get to that destination? If you're running a $25 million business and you want a $50 million business, what do you need to make the leap? If you're serving 5000 clients per week, how could you serve 10,000?

Return to the nine building blocks and consider what needs to happen in each area of your business:

- *Customer segments* – which customers do you want to be targeting? Is this the same group you currently target, or do you want to reach a new segment?
- *Value propositions* – do you intend to offer the same products and services, or do you want to branch into new areas? What is the distinctive promise you're making?
- *Channels* – if you want to reach more customers, how might you do this? Is there a new channel to develop?
- *Customer relationships* – if you want to reach more customers, how might this impact your relationships? Will you need more automation?
- *Revenue streams* – are you creating new revenue streams and, if so, how will these be managed?
- *Key resources* – what resources will you need to achieve your goals? Will these be sourced from within the business, or will you source them externally?
- *Key activities* – what major activities will you need to action for differentiation?
- *Key partners* – when it comes to the key resources and activities you will source externally, who can help you with these?
- *Cost structure* – how will you manage the costs associated with growth? Where are the savings to be made?

Working through the Business Model Canvas is an invaluable exercise for my clients who are seeking to articulate their business model, allowing them to take stock of 'where they are today'. It is rare that they have thought about their business in this way, identifying areas of opportunity, key dependencies and risks, and their weighting on particular streams of revenue or cost.

In the case of a client who's a major fruit grower, the scale of his operations dictates that much of his produce gets sold into the major supermarket chains and the export market. But the side effect is that the high specifications of these key customers drives a large volume of 'seconds' or waste fruit. In a different model that focused on selling solely through a wholesale market channel, this would not be such a big issue as the standards are different. But for my client to optimise his model there is now a strategic imperative around innovation to profitably use the seconds fruit.

Of particular benefit are the customer-related aspects of the exercise, which underscores the importance of what I discussed in part II of this book around understanding your customers. I find time and again that it is only when clients think deeply about what the customer is trying to get done, what pains they experience in pursuing these goals and what gains they are seeking to achieve, that they reach a clear understanding of customer expectations and the actual competencies, capabilities and value their company brings to the customer. I am literally encouraging the client to 'walk a mile in their customer's shoes' to consider the products and services they have put into the market and the role they are playing in relieving pains and delivering gains – and discovering if they are a match.

PROPELLER TIP: With everything you know about your customer needs and the trends shaping the market, consider what model a complete outsider to the industry would use.

This exercise is a challenging mental leap for many business leaders. Their success has frequently been built on the profile of the founder or leader or the products and services they have created, and for which they have become well known in their market. In the first instance, standing on the other side of the fence, ignoring what they do and thinking solely about the customer is very revealing about important gaps they may not be serving, as well as the things they are doing which are no longer relevant to their client base.

For my clients, using tools such as this to get a better insight into how the 'machine' of their business works has been crucial in making more informed decisions. In one instance it helped the whole leadership team realise just how dependent they were on a single government client that provided seventy per cent of their revenue, so they quickly moved to diversify their revenue streams before that major contract ended. In another case for a commercial contracting firm, the current channels they had were not going to deliver the $40m revenue growth we'd projected over the coming three years. The strategy and associated near-term priorities now reflect a push to develop new interstate markets.

Comparing models against competitors and industry benchmarks has also helped clients to move the needle on their product/service mix: one client found that their most profitable line of business represented only 2.5 per cent of revenue. With renewed focus, that number has already been lifted to 3.75 per cent (that is, has gone up fifty per cent) and the founder has set his team the challenge of getting it to ten per cent. This is how leaders shift the needle: objectively understanding how things are working now, what they could or should be, and deciding how to make that change happen.

* * *

Understanding the needs of your customers is the foundation on which the other building blocks of a business model are built. It allows you to build an architecture around the value proposition your products and services provide, selecting the channels that help you deliver them, tapping into new revenue streams, putting into place necessary resources, and undertaking the activities required to achieve your goals, finding the right partners to support your activities and managing the costs associated with growth.

Once you've gained clarity in all nine areas of the Business Model Canvas, you are ready to undertake the final step in the Conceive stage: understanding and managing the risks involved as you begin to transform your business.

KEY POINTS

1. Your business model describes how you match your capabilities to the needs of your target market.
2. Many businesses have never thought about their business model or struggle to articulate it beyond basic terms.
3. Mapping out a clear business model will help identify areas of the business that require focus and alignment to deliver your strategy.
4. Use the Business Model Canvas to assess the structure, resources, partners and activities (and related costs) your business provides to deliver its value proposition. On the other side of the model are the customer relationships, channels and segments (and related revenue streams) that a business attracts from delivering its value proposition.
5. Understanding the business models used by competitors can help highlight areas to differentiate your own.

TAKE ACTION

What is your current business model? Does it need to change? Consider the nine building blocks of the Business Model Canvas, then ask yourself these questions:

1. How will your business model need to change to best leverage your competencies and fulfil the highest needs of your core customers?
2. Which areas of your business model provide the highest future scaling potential?

3. What do your competitor or substitute models look like? Where is your edge over them? (And what is their edge over you?)
4. How strong is your model and how long do you expect it to provide an advantage?
5. Where are the risks and how could you protect your most critical business model elements?

CHAPTER 9

Risk management

'Take risks. Ask big questions. Don't be afraid to make mistakes; if you don't make mistakes, you're not reaching far enough.'

David Packard, co-founder of Hewlett-Packard

BE PREPARED

My client's annual offsite strategy retreat started in its usual cordial fashion. This cohesive team runs a high-tech manufacturing business that sells its products around the world and has built a solid reputation over four decades. As the morning progressed I started to pull out some of the challenges they'd faced through the past year and noticed a theme: a key client threatening to leave, a lack of reliability in the product suite, challenges managing projects, a shortage of key technical people. It became a long list, so I suggested we change the agenda and dig into some of the fundamentals. A robust, open and honest conversation followed, yielding several causes for the range of challenges they'd faced:

- they had established a new factory in Asia
- a new core technology was being used in their major product range

- production volumes had significantly risen
- the product range had expanded
- a cost-cutting initiative had seen a shift to some lower quality components.

Each of these decisions was independently sound, but together the compound effect was giving them some serious headaches.

As humans, we have a natural bias that leads us to we assume that we're right. As a result, we tend not to look closely enough at risks. For a business, this can be a fatal mistake, although happily for my client, having made the issues and risks visible, and having the courage to have a very robust leadership discussion, we were able to take fast corrective action.

Research by Dr John Kotter into strategic failure found that seventy per cent of strategic business initiatives failed to meet their objectives.[1] While careful planning can help avoid such failure, unforeseen circumstances can derail even the best laid plans. However, what sets businesses apart when things go wrong is the evaluation and preparation they have undertaken to manage risk.

Successful risk management involves recognising that a strategy might not yield the results you hope for, or, if it does, that there can be unexpected internal and external business factors that can cause blips along the way.

Businesses that don't prepare for risk are vulnerable should problems arise, and the consequences could include losing profits, customers, staff and partners. Ultimately, your business's reputation could also be damaged or the business itself could be lost. Think about what would happen if there were a three-day power outage in your area, or if your largest customer went bust, or if a staff member

1 John Kotter, *Leading Change*.

embezzled $500,000. How would that impact on your business? For some, an event like that would spell the end.

If you were prepared for those risks, however, the consequences wouldn't be as severe. If there were a three-day power outage, you might have an alternate venue where your key people could keep things running. If your largest customer went bust, you might have already started building relationships with other potential customers. In the case of embezzlement, being prepared could both reduce the potential of this risk occurring, insure for it, and detect any fraud that does occur early, which would reduce the financial loss.

STRATEGIC RISK MANAGEMENT

Sensible risk management is not about creating a culture of micromanagement where every new idea is met with 'no'. However, it is prudent commercial sense to run everything through a well-considered filter so that you can avoid nasty surprises. If you actively manage risks, you can avoid, accept, transfer or mitigate almost any that eventuate.

Risk identification

To manage the risks to your strategy, the first step is simply identifying any potential risks. These include both those inherent in your strategy and external factors that could have an impact. These could include:

- *Customers* – what happens if a significant customer leaves?
- *Suppliers* – how dependent are you on a single supplier of a critical component?
- *Partners* – how reliable are your partnership arrangements, such as those with your bankers or product distributors?
- *Staff* – what is your dependence on key staff (which may include the founder or owner)?

- *Products or services* – does your design, manufacturing or distribution expose your business to risk? Would the loss of a design or a right, say through an IP breach, cause a problem?
- *Infrastructure* – how reliant are you on infrastructure, such as information technology?
- *Regulatory* – does your business rely on regulatory conditions? What if laws or rules change, such as minimum wage rates or compliance requirements?
- *Economic* – how exposed is your business to interest rates, exchange rates, or the health of other economies with which you trade?

In each of these categories, ask yourself what could go wrong. Typically, the risk is higher when you are dealing with a new scenario (such as a new supplier or product), or when there are large amounts of time, money or other assets at stake (such as with a large customer or significant partner).

Risk assessment

Once you have a list of risks, the next step is to assess them, considering both the likelihood of the risk happening and the impact if it were to happen. The likelihood may range from very likely to unlikely. The impact may range from causing major damage to minor or negligible consequences.

Should a risk eventuate, it could also impact your business in a number of areas (and, in the worst-case scenario, every area). These could include:

- *Financial* – what might the bottom line impact of a certain risk be?
- *Time* – could delays cause your business to lose momentum or an entire opportunity?

- *People* – how might you lose the trust of your staff, customers and suppliers?
- *Physical* – could a key building or vital equipment be lost?
- *Legal* – is there potential for you to be tied up in an expensive, stressful, distracting legal case?
- *Reputation* – could your corporate brand or personal reputations suffer critical damage?

To evaluate the impact of the risks you listed previously, simply rate the likelihood of each risk as 'very likely' (it is almost certain that this risk will occur several times a year), 'likely' (strong possibility it will happen in any given year) or 'unlikely' (not expected but still a possibility), and the impact of each risk as 'minor' (this may include minor injuries, a brief system outage, short-lived inconvenience), 'moderate' (multiple staff days lost, client dissatisfaction, adverse media) or 'major' (death, disability, lengthy outages of key systems, significant financial implications).

Next, use these ratings to plot each risk on a risk assessment matrix, as shown below. While this is obviously not intended to be a detailed actuarial exercise, it will help you determine the severity of each risk.

Risk assessment matrix

Likelihood
How likely is the risk?

Very likely	**Medium**	**High**	**Extreme**
Likely	**Low**	**Medium**	**High**
Unlikely	**Low**	**Low**	**Medium**
	Minor	Moderate	Major

Impact
How serious is the risk?

Risk management

Once you have identified and evaluated the impact of the risks to your strategy, the final step is determining how these risks should be managed. There are four ways to manage risks:

1. *Avoidance* – changing the strategy because the risk is so great that you'd rather avoid it entirely.
2. *Acceptance* – accepting the risk because the impact and likelihood are both very low, or within commercial tolerances.
3. *Transfer* – outsourcing responsibility for the risk (for example, getting insurance, or taking on a partner to share both the upside and downside).
4. *Mitigation* – investment in a solution for the risk, such as server duplication or additional team members or capital equipment.

How you respond to each risk will be guided by each risk's rating. For example, if a risk has an Extreme rating, it means that risk is almost sure to happen and will have dire consequences. In this case you would want to immediately contain the risk, putting measures in place to reduce its likelihood and impact. By contrast, if a risk has a Low rating, that risk is unlikely to eventuate, and even if it did it would have minor or negligible consequences. In this case you might decide that mitigating the risk is more trouble than simply responding to it should it occur.

It's essential to be clear on the risks you are exposed to and how much risk you can accept. Once you know these two elements, you can decide on your approach. Return to your list of risks and start by deciding which ones need to be addressed, and which you are happy to accept. Depending on the nature of your business, you may be willing to accept a Low to Medium level of risk, which means you only need to address the items rated as High or Extreme. Or you might be in an area where your risk tolerance is extremely low, so you need to do as much as possible to mitigate every risk.

Once you have made a shortlist of each risk that needs to be addressed, ask yourself and your team these questions. First, how can the risk be avoided? What can you do today to prevent this risk from occurring? What can you put in place to track that a risk is emerging? What can you do if it does occur? Is there any way to lessen the potential damage?

Let's consider the protection of data as an issue faced by most businesses. If you don't have a backup of your data, the risk is potentially losing everything should a fire, virus, fraud, or any number of other incidents occur. While the likelihood might not be high, the impact would be major, so we're looking at a Medium to High risk.

Your options for mitigating that risk then come down to how you back up the data. Let's say option one is offsite storage that is updated weekly – this means that if you have a fire, you'll only lose one week of data. In some businesses that might be an acceptable level of risk, while others might feel that the impact of losing one week's data would be too damaging. If you're in the second group, your next option might be dual writing, whereby as soon as you save something onsite it is backed up in the cloud.

The next thing to consider is the impact of your mitigation strategy from a time, money and people perspective. How much will it cost to use this method? How long will it take? How many of your people are required? This will help you determine the return of each risk mitigation option.

To return to the data backup issue, you might have the option to have every transaction backed up in real time to three places offshore in the cloud as an expensive premium solution. Another option might be backing everything up once a day for half the price. Given the expense of backing up everything in real time, and the fact that you wouldn't lose significant data in a single day, you might conclude that – based on the required investment, the likelihood of the risk and the impact of the risk – you are happy to spend half the amount and have the daily backup. The point is that you're making an informed choice.

In the case of one of my clients who have a hi-tech manufacturing operation, we developed a growth strategy that involved the sale of a key product component they had created to a network of international equipment manufacturers. Undertaking a careful risk examination, they determined that intellectual property (IP) was a significant concern, given there was a moderate likelihood their design could be copied by other manufacturers if they failed to secure the necessary patent on the product. The impact would be severe, given the amount of revenue they stood to lose. Accordingly, I referred them to a specialist IP lawyer to introduce the relevant protections, thereby mitigating the potential risk.

PROPELLER TIP: Be aware of the compounding effect of decisions, rather than just the standalone risk of each independent decision.

Monitoring and review

The final element of risk management is monitoring and reviewing your risk plan. This includes keeping necessary records and reviewing your risk plan against your business's experiences at regular intervals so you can make changes as necessary.

The key is to do this regularly, based on the nature of the risks. Some may be slow-moving while others are rapid. The other time to review is when you have a trigger event; for example, the resignation of a key staff member, acquisition of a new business or significant contract, or a new strategic initiative such as releasing a new product or entering a new territory.

In this regard, it's instructive to reflect on the story of Lehman Brothers during 2008's global financial crisis (GFC). Despite a supposed culture of risk management, and the governance systems and processes to make it work, what seemed an extremely unlikely event (a substantial increase in mortgage defaults) was actually predictable and had been brewing for some time. The risk kept escalating and the company was seemingly blind to it. We all know how this ended.

As I finalise this edit of my book, the world is deep in the grip of COVID-19. Like the GFC, the ripples from the initial source, due to the interconnectedness of the modern world, were fast and widespread. It has been interesting to watch the differing responses that ranged from complete elimination, to various forms of suppression, through to the more Darwinian approaches (do nothing and let it play out with natural immunity). A remarkable feature of this event has been the continual referral to it being 'unprecedented', when in fact we had a significant precedent with the Spanish Flu one hundred years earlier, and we experienced a close relation of COVID-19, SARS, from 2003. The reality, though, is that most businesses would not have had an event like this on their risk matrix and accordingly were under-prepared. I imagine that most will now have a broader view of risk as few organisations will have escaped COVID-19 unscathed. As leaders, though, will we absorb the lesson and adopt better risk practices or will this be just an event that is relatively soon forgotten?

By clarifying, evaluating and mitigating your risk, and monitoring risks over time, you will be comfortable to launch full steam ahead into activating your strategy.

KEY POINTS

1. Risk management is one of the foundations of good governance.
2. The reality is that there are likely numerous risk blind spots in your business right now.
3. Any potential risks, both inherent in your strategy and external factors that could impact on your strategy, need to be anticipated, evaluated and managed.
4. A framework needs to be established to support structured assessment of risk on an ongoing basis.
5. Your business needs to accept risk-taking as part of growth, yet confidently call out the concerns.

TAKE ACTION

If you haven't had a rigorous risk-based approach until now, what is your business's current risk profile? Now consider:

1. What is the biggest threat to your current business that requires prompt attention?
2. What are the underlying trends – say, in the economy, demographics or technology – that affect the likelihood or impact of any of your risks?
3. What could go wrong with your intended strategies? Are you spread too thin and not sufficiently backing your strongest plays? Can cash flow keep up with your speed of growth?
4. How will you avoid, transfer or mitigate potential risks? Are there some risks you are willing to accept?
5. Where are the areas where you should be taking *more* risk?

PART IV
Activation

'Plans are only good intentions unless they immediately degenerate into hard work.'

Peter Drucker, management theorist

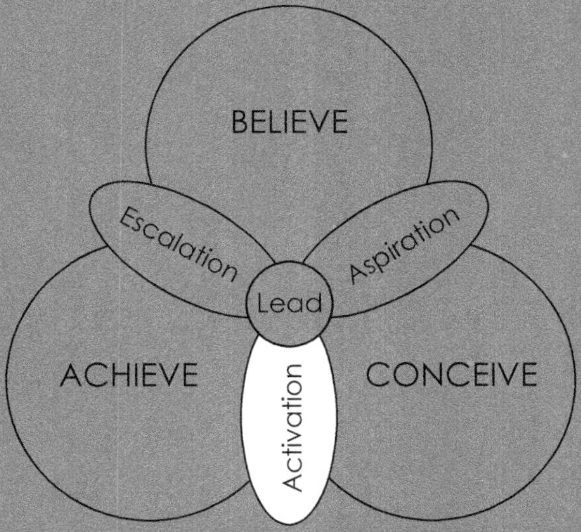

ACTIVATION is how you connect your strategy, the *Conceive* stage, into your business and the enablers that need to be put in place to implement the strategy (the *Achieve* stage). During *Activation*, you translate your thinking into action by sharing your strategy with your people. As they will be carrying it out, the way your team receives this strategy will be a demonstration of their commitment. At this stage, it is also critical to be clear about accountability for delivering on the agreed priorities, and to declare the measures that will track progress.

CHAPTER 10

Accountability

'An organisation's ability to learn,
and translate that learning into action rapidly,
is the ultimate competitive advantage.'

Jack Welch, former CEO of General Electric

You've doubtless seen this issue at some point: somewhere between your team euphorically agreeing to this year's strategic initiatives and actually implementing them, enthusiasm wanes. People dither and drift, and somehow get drawn back into their day-to-day responsibilities while your strategy gathers dust in the bottom of a drawer.

What happened to the team commitment you thought you had? Was your strategy flawed? Did you have the wrong people on board? Were they struggling with performance anxiety?

If you've struggled with these issues at some point, you're not alone. According to consultant William Schieman, a contributing author to the book *Performance Management: Putting Research into Action*, while sixty-five per cent of businesses have an agreed strategy, only fourteen per cent of employees actually understand it, and *less than ten per cent* of businesses successfully execute it.[1]

---

1 James W. Smither and Manuel London (eds), *Performance Management: Putting Research into Action* (Pfeiffer, 2009).

In my view, there are three key reasons for these deplorable statistics:

- there is often a failure to assign and accept accountability for key priorities
- there is no measure of success
- there are typically shortcomings in communication.

It's important to consider each one of these items in turn, so that you can successfully share your strategy with your team and translate your thinking into action.

NINETY-DAY GOALS

In the earlier Strategy chapter of this book, you undertook the important work of devising your three-to-five-year and one-year strategies. But how do you ensure they are put into action, stay on track, and that your people and teams are kept accountable for them? The important next step that is a key insight from *Scaling Up* is what most businesses miss: quickly determining the relevant priorities for the next ninety days, identifying the key performance indicators, and agreeing accountabilities for action.

Your ninety-day goal should detail the actions, ideas, and policies you need to create, and the resources required to support each of these within that timeframe. This milestone not only makes your bigger objectives more attainable, but starts to add the actionable detail that is commonly missing from the broad goals often passed off as 'strategies'.

PROPELLER TIP: Momentum is built from clear priorities in fast ninety-day cycles, with specific, outcome-oriented accountabilities taken by key leaders.

So, when it comes to where your business is going, what could you achieve over the next ninety days to make progress towards your yearly and three-to-five-year strategies? What are the milestones you need to reach?

First, consider the activities that may be necessary. There are a handful of what I call 'action groups' that activities commonly fall under:

- *Research* – what knowledge does your business need to reach your ninety-day goal? Do you need to complete any feasibility studies to determine your course of action?
- *Development* – which systems and processes need to be developed to achieve your goal? Are these developments required to support the growth of your existing products and services, create new ones, or enable the back office?
- *Connections* – who can you connect with to help you achieve your goal? Do you have existing relationships with partners and suppliers, or do you need to establish a new partnership to reach your goal?
- *Customers* – what do you need to reach a new customer segment or expand in your existing segment? If your goal is to open in a new market, how can you reach that market?

Once you've decided on the necessary activities, you will need to marshal your resources to carry them out.

For instance, a development activity might be implementing a new system for customer relationship management (CRM). This activity would then have smaller sub-activities, like researching the different CRMs available for businesses of your size; doing a cost–benefit analysis for each, including using internal resources for installation or an external team; and understanding the training program required to get the CRM up and running throughout your business. When creating the initial high-level plan though, just focus on the major activities required for each area. What are the headline objectives/key results within this period?

After establishing the high-level activities required in each area with your leadership team, the next step is to consult the relevant teams in each part of the business (or the relevant key people, keeping in mind that your organisational structure may need to change to support your strategy), to be clear on the largest sub-activities that come under each of the major activities.

Finally, you can use these sub-activities to determine the resources you'll need to carry out your strategy. Assess the resources your business currently has available, and the gap between what you have now and what you need to achieve the ninety-day goal. So think about:

- What capabilities does your business need to develop to achieve your ninety-day goal?
- What other resources (financial, people and physical) do you need to develop to achieve this?
- Do all of these resources and capabilities need to be sourced internally, or are there external partners who can help?

By condensing your annual priorities into a small set of ninety-day goals, and then breaking this into these sub-activities, it will be easier for you and your leadership team to determine priorities and allocate resources. It will also be easier to communicate the strategy across the business and keep people accountable along the way.

ASSIGNING ACCOUNTABILITY

'Accountability breeds response-ability.'

Stephen Covey

When it comes to assigning accountability, make sure that *only one person* is accountable for each priority, even if a number of people are involved in working on it. If not, it's the same old story of 'if everyone is accountable, no-one is accountable', and nothing important gets done.

Once you have assigned accountability, you need to set very clear expectations about what's involved in delivering on each priority. Your team needs to be committed to them, and the accountable individuals need to have the capability, time and resources to get them done, and must be prepared to delegate if they do not.

One company where I have seen accountability drive rapid improvement is with my client Ecotech, a global leader in the design, manufacture, operation and maintenance of environmental monitoring systems. Each year, the company's annual priorities provide inspiration for, in the first instance, a set of ninety-day priorities, which are then split into individual priorities proposed by each of the executive team members. The team then comes together to engage in a robust discussion around these quarterly priorities before agreeing on and committing to them. While they agree the 'Top 5' for the business, each executive is given sole accountability for their own priorities, and clear expectations are set for the delivery of them.

By having these clear expectations, each executive leader can assess the time and resources required to achieve them, and put the necessary support into place among their own teams. And by publicly agreeing to the priorities in front of their peers, they feel a greater sense of accountability, knowing that each quarter their pledges will later be revisited around the same table. Over years of doing this with clients I've found that individuals get about seventy-five per cent of their accountabilities delivered each quarter, which I see as a nice balance between the accountabilities having been too easy (they regularly get everything done) and too ambitious (where they get nothing done).

When it comes to reviewing progress at quarter's end, it's great leadership for the most senior leader to show the way in declaring the state of their quarterly priorities: green means priority achieved, orange means a near miss but almost there, while red is for everything else. This approach gives permission, and an expectation, for the rest of your team to be honest too. This colour-coding system is much better than the vague and excuse-laden discussions that I imagine most non-performing teams have. Frankly, I've been pleasantly surprised how quickly my client teams have embraced this truth-telling exercise. For any doubters, there are real benefits from recognising all the green ticks against the achievements, and the red crosses provide an important opportunity for a valuable discussion. Did we lack the time, focus or capability to deliver on that priority? Is it still important this coming quarter?

This came up for a client who'd fallen short in their quarterly priority around business development into a set of targeted prospects. While they are deep functional experts in their professional field, a bit of exploratory questioning revealed that they lacked skill and confidence to translate this into sales. Stepping up revenue was a clear 'front domino' for these guys and, accordingly, the next set of quarterly priorities included referring them to a professional to build capability in sales. The principle here reinforces an insight from my coach training many years ago: 'Performance = Potential – Interference'. Use the quarterly priority-setting to work through the 'interferences' inside your business to make it all run a bit more elegantly for you as a leader and more easily for those on your team.

For all of the businesses I work with, once their senior leaders are comfortable and confident with the process of establishing ninety-day goals with required activities, priorities and accountabilities, I coach them to roll it out with their own teams in the same manner. When they emulate the process and have their team agree on their plans together, it helps to 'depersonalise' discussions down the track when it comes to reviewing progress through the month. That is, reviews are based on the goals the team members themselves committed to, making it easier for the leader to provide support and constructive feedback around the objectives and current results, rather than the employee feeling like they are receiving personal criticism. This feedback model is also far more timely and useful than a traditional annual performance review.

You need to have a similarly rigorous process in place in your business to ensure that responsibility for different priorities is not handballed between team members, which can lead to a culture of finger-pointing when things go wrong. When a clear line of accountability exists, people will know exactly what's expected of them and can commit to delivering their goals before their performance is reviewed as a team further down the track.

My tip is to start simple, especially if accountability-taking is new, by just getting your people to agree to take on a task and report back on progress. Once this is done, you can add more detail to different priorities, include tighter measures of success, and fully roll out your ninety-day goals. Later, once they've become used to the rhythm, you'll find that you can stretch your people a bit more, and you'll feel the real lift when they start challenging each other.

KEY POINTS

1. Assigning accountability is where you translate strategic thinking into near-term action.
2. Lack of accountability is a key failure point for strategic success.
3. The result of poor accountability is seen in a lack of delivery on key priorities.
4. Having clear alignment of priorities, so everyone knows what's important, is critical.
5. Implementing a system for agreeing and reviewing accountabilities brings it to life through building commitment.

TAKE ACTION

Do you have a strong enough approach to get your priorities actioned? Consider these points:

1. Can you clearly articulate your annual strategy into ninety-day priorities?
2. Before burying you team in work, how would you rate their capability to deliver on these priorities? (Is there a risk that you'll attempt the impossible?)
3. What first steps will you take to build a culture of accountability with your team?
4. How about the system for tracking it? Will you do regular check-in meetings or track progress online?
5. What is the history of accountability-taking? Have you unfairly criticised employees who were lumped with an impossible task? Or perhaps you've praised certain team members while ignoring the unsung heroes? How will you make sure accountability is done fairly?

CHAPTER 11

Measurement

'Tell me how you measure me,
and I will tell you how I will behave.'

Eliyahu M. Goldratt, business management theorist

WHAT ARE THE VITAL SIGNS FOR YOUR BUSINESS?

In terms of measurement, what will success look like to you? As Verne Hamish shared in *Scaling Up*, what are the critical numbers that you need to hit this month, quarter or year? How are you casting an eye to the future to look at the prospective fortunes of your business? And how will you keep track of performance in real time?

In a sense, you need to consider your business in the same way that an emergency room doctor considers an incoming patient. Before you is a complex organism. While there are many things going on and many things you *could* measure, what are the vital signs that tell you how the underlying system is performing? In the case of an ER patient, this will include their heart rate, temperature, respiration and blood pressure. For you and your business, what will those critical few metrics be?

Clearly defining your goals with a form of measurement has three benefits. First, everyone has the same picture of success.

For instance, instead of 'a stronger focus on sales', the measure of success is '$2 million in additional sales in our Southern Region.' The expectation is clear. Recall the run-rate examples that I wrote about earlier in the book: the professional services client seeking $10k/week in additional sales or the commercial contracting client growing at twenty per cent per annum. They have a benchmark to measure against and hold themselves accountable to.

Second, you can monitor your progress and celebrate when you achieve critical numbers. We should have measures and indicators on three time dimensions: historical, so that we can see how our decisions played out, and appropriately recognise, reward and celebrate; current time, so that we can check on the health of our functions, processes and priorities to get a sense of operational and strategic wellbeing; and future – we should have sensors that tell us in advance about pending operational or strategic issues. Think about a car and the number of things the dashboard might tell us: the odometer for our history of distance travelled, the speedo and tacho for how hard the car is working right now, and the service due indicator telling us when we'll need to get attention.

The third, and perhaps least obvious benefit, is that having a challenging goal is a litmus test of your people and culture. In a growth-oriented business, you need people who will thrive on positive challenges, and this is one way to determine organisational appetite. In a healthy growth culture, people will actively seek this challenge in the same way that professional sports stars strive for an Olympic medal or major league titles.

SCOREBOARDS

My biggest insight on the power of visible metrics was a visit to SRC in Springfield, Missouri. Jack Stack has been driving the performance culture at SRC since he and a couple of colleagues bought out the plant from the failing International Harvester Company in the early 1980s. Their foundational business was reconditioning heavy-duty engines for trucks and agricultural machinery, and their success has seen that original enterprise blossom into a range of other industries. One of Jack's key insights was that people love games and winning, and in their recreation time they'll often be playing or watching sport. In that regard, he saw business as just another type of game (hence the title of his book is *The Great Game of Business*), and yet most businesses do not operate with that mindset: as leaders, we haven't taught our teams the rules, given them a playbook or showed them the score ... can you imagine going along to your favourite sporting event and not being able to see the scoreboard? How bizarre (and unengaging) would that be? And yet mostly that is how businesses operate.

In SRC's case, everyone is taught how success is measured and there are metrics everywhere around their factories and offices: detailed, full-wall balance sheets, profit and loss statements and cash flow statements, lost time injury records, products shipped run-rate, awards won, progress towards bonus. There are returned products on benches with defects tagged for staff to see and learn. In the SRC Electrical plant that I visited, all 160 staff get into the training room every Thursday for thirty minutes to participate in projecting performance for the remainder of each month. The takeaway is that there are lots of ways that SRC's team members get an insight into how the business has been going and where it is going, and accordingly where the effort needs to be directed.

PROPELLER TIP: Get scoreboards up so that everyone can see how they are tracking.

How could you introduce this sort of metrics-based approach into your business? Watch the behaviours of your team when you start measuring the key numbers. It will speak volumes about the individuals and your prospects for growth. While the standout performers will quickly become apparent, it will also highlight underperformers who may have previously gone under the radar. Some leaders may want to avoid the uncomfortable conversations that can follow such revelations, but it's important to think of this as a chance to provide constructive feedback and make improvements.

It's sometimes the fear of this reaction that holds leaders back from being definitive about the numbers – sure, it leaves an escape route, but it also means that the opportunity for clarity, alignment and learning escapes too.

It certainly doesn't happen that way for my clients. A surprise to some will be the relatively limited focus that my fast-growth clients have on the financials. While they are obviously important, they realise that the financials are the *result* of everything else that has been done, not the precursor. You can't simply declare your intention to increase revenue and expect it to magically happen; you need to attract prospects into your sales funnel, convert them into signed contracts, and then deliver.

In a governance sense, being clear about the health of your profit and loss statement, balance sheet and cash flow is crucial, especially for fast-growth entities where cash is being used quickly in staffing, technology, and inventory, while the cash inflow from increasingly large customers may slow down. And as markets develop, the margins usually tighten. Accordingly, the figures need to be reviewed on three horizons: historical performance, current performance (especially cash flow), and future projections.

In addition to the core financials, I like to get clients thinking about a key priority for the quarter – something that will be a significant driving force in their overall success in this immediate timeframe. A great example comes from my client Dimple. When we reviewed an upcoming quarter, it was clear that recent sales had been going extremely well, and this flow of new work could be profiled against staffing numbers. It became apparent that several new clinical staff would need to be added to the team to serve these contracts as they became operational. Leadership team insight: winning more work wasn't the key issue but staffing the work was. So a clinical staff recruiting target became the critical number for the leadership team to measure success against.

MEASURING YOUR RESOURCES

The other valuable dividend from measuring things is that you can better evaluate resource allocation. As we learned in the Conceive section, we have to make choices about our strategy, the business model choices to deliver it, and our level of risk-taking along the way. When these decisions are actually up and running, we need to keep track of their performance.

In this regard, we can learn something from Pixar. Chances are, especially if you have children younger than twenty-five, the film studio's animated productions have been on your watched list: *Toy Story*, *Finding Nemo*, *A Bug's Life*, *Monsters, Inc.*, to name a few. Pixar President Ed Catmull describes in his book *Creativity, Inc.* that each of the company's masterpieces takes about 22,000 person-weeks of effort, through which everyone is 'just trying to make a better movie'.[1] As the boss of Pixar and later Disney Animation, his challenge was to corral his extraordinary army of creative minds to deliver remarkable productions...but within realistic limits.

---

1 Ed Catmull, *Creativity, Inc* (Transworld Publishers, 2014).

To force prioritisation between competing ideas, Catmull oversaw the introduction of a novel method whereby directors could visually keep track of each person-week. A set number of popsicle sticks – each representing a person-week of work – were stuck up onto a board and arranged so that the directors could clearly see how many weeks each part of their movie was taking. If a director wanted to speed up production by adding new person-weeks to their film, they would have to take sticks from somewhere else. Not only did this make it easy to keep track of how resources were being allocated, it ensured that teams weren't promising more than they could deliver.

Is there some sort of measurement system you could use that shows whether all your 'popsicle sticks' are lined up for best effect? Thinking about your key drivers of cost, could you use a system like this to communicate limits and measure inputs on your retail-store rollout, new product release, patient-care initiative, technical-support program, sustainability project, and so forth?

HOW DO YOU MONITOR TRENDS?

While it's important to have a sense of what's operationally going on now, and what the financial results were for previous months, it's also crucial to keep an eye on the future. For the US$100 billion engineering and electronics giant Bosch, this means monitoring the mega-trends in their industry and predicting their impact. For instance, despite the advances they made with their turbochargers that increase fuel efficiency, the company recognised that the steady advance of electric vehicles would eventually force those products out of the market, so they decided to sell that arm of the business. They also exited their solar PV business in the face of plummeting prices. According to Gavin Smith, President of Robert Bosch (Australia), the company uses the information it gathers about future trends to 'eat its own children and shoot its ancestors' – that is, they watch for market signals and sell out where they can.

How do you track the impact of trends in your world? What was the last venture you killed in response to a trend change, and how did you decide which one it was? Scoring out of ten, how would you rate your leadership group's record of confronting the brutal facts to make these important decisions?

* * *

Now that you're clear on the key drivers of success for your team to focus on, are tracking real-time measures of performance and making necessary adjustments, and have a telescope looking into the future to help make some early judgements, it's time to turn your attention to the vital role that communication plays in your business.

KEY POINTS

1. Measurement is critical to providing feedback on our decisions.
2. It is difficult to foster accountability with no measure of performance, and most businesses are too light on useful decision-oriented measures.
3. The result is uninformed decisions, missed opportunities and lacklustre performance.
4. The key is to create measures for the past, the present and projections.
5. A dashboard of measures is needed across finances, operations and strategic priorities.

TAKE ACTION

Have you got the right measures of business health? Consider these points:

1. For your most important priority, how are you measuring progress?
2. Thinking about operations, what are the things that tell you that the 'machine' of your business is working (or not)?
3. With the financials, is it all considered to be historical information, or is it presented so you can make real-time decisions?
4. For emergent issues or risks, how are they being tracked to avoid you being blindsided?
5. How can you best keep the key measures in front of your people?

CHAPTER 12

Communication

'Effective communication is twenty per cent what you know and eighty per cent how you feel about what you know.'

Jim Rohn, business entrepreneur

SHARING YOUR PLANS AND STRATEGY

Communication is a vital, if overlooked, part of the strategic process. Most of the time, strategic communication is ineffective at best and damaging at worst. Like a game of Chinese whispers, it's easy for the message to get mutated as it travels from the top of the organisation to the shop floor. The way the strategy is miscommunicated often means individuals can't see what's in it for them, and how the overall strategy relates to their role. Often the leadership team try to share the entire strategy, which results in the detail becoming overwhelming for those who don't need to understand every complexity. And, finally, when the leadership team invites debate, you may find a reduction in commitment to the strategy.

I suspect that part of the problem also emanates from leaders being self-conscious about standing at the front of a room, probably made worse because they lack personal clarity or confidence in the message to be shared. Happily, the work that has been done in preceding sections of this book has provided all the core elements regarding the why, where, what and how that will underpin the story you tell. Ultimately, then, leaders need to address three areas: the method of communication, the amount of detail they include, and the timing.

Choosing the right communication methods

In a study of more than 60,000 responses to a global employee-satisfaction survey spanning over 300 companies, Immanuel Hermreck, a leadership professor at INSEAD, and Charles Galunic, the head of human resources at Bertelsmann, found that top management had the most significant impact on how well employees grasp and support strategy.[1] The impact of senior management was far greater than any other variable examined.

As a result, a 'cascade' method, where senior leaders communicate strategy to their direct reports and depend on them to share it with the rest of the business, is often ineffective, creating more opportunities for the message to get lost in translation, and fewer opportunities for employees to join the debate.

The most effective way to communicate strategy is through the senior managers themselves. A presentation is one way, but reciprocal exchanges that also allow employees to have their voices heard are more effective. This helps you and your leadership team to remain involved in what's happening on the ground level as your business grows. My client Gaethan Cutri has done this well through setting up a corporate WhatsApp group for his Cutri Fruit team through which he regularly appears on video sharing his views on the organisational strategy, examples of values alignment and key operational matters. One of his videos was announcing their strategic theme of 'Make the

---

1 Charles Galunic and Immanuel Hermreck, 'How to Help Employees "Get" Strategy', *Harvard Business Review*, December 1, 2012. hbr.org/2012/12/how-to-help-employees-get-strategy.

Grade' that we agreed during the annual planning meeting. The theme has been a handy communications tool because it is short and sharp, but also speaks strongly to what they need to deliver to their customer (top-grade fruit) and how each individual must act in their own role to make that happen (top-grade performance).

Yes, there is a discipline to do things like this and a regular cadence is required, remembering that people rarely hear the message you want to communicate the first time around. Furthermore, if your business has a history of announcing new strategies and initiatives without implementing them, your people will assume it's just another fad that will never lead anywhere. Plus, we all interpret via our own lens 'what does this mean for me/my team/my customers ... '

This is why it's essential to continue to reinforce your strategy beyond the initial presentation or round tables. This might include regular email updates, information leaflets, a staff chatroom or a social media group where they can ask questions, and meetings regarding the role each team will play.

The result of hearing about the strategy from the leaders of your business in person, then having it reinforced through various channels over the following weeks and months, is that people at all levels 'buy in' and start investing in it with their time and expertise.

One of my clients, a mid-tier law firm, holds an annual event for their Corporate and Commercial department, so that the heads of the division can communicate the strategy for the year ahead and get the team involved in shaping plans for the practice.

There are then quarterly review meetings for the senior team members, and they have adopted weekly whole-of-team meetings to check on progress. These meetings are in a dedicated space where they have the walls covered in the content they've created so that the team can easily stay in touch with the purpose, values and annual goals of the business. They then write the top five strategic priorities across a giant whiteboard at one end of the room, with task breakdowns under each priority and columns for 'to be done', 'doing' and 'done'. This makes it very easy for everyone on the team to get a visual image on how things are going. They've also made it a bit fun and quirky by having cartoon caricatures of each person in the team stuck on a magnet so that they can move their character across the magnetic board as their individual tasks get done (and, in front of all your peers, do you want to be the person who's character hasn't moved on the board?).

The strategies are further reinforced by each of the practice's principals coaching a couple of staff with a one-on-one meeting every month. This is an opportunity to check in with each person on how they are going with their part of the plan and to help with any 'stucks'.

I've introduced the same ideas to my client Daniel Crawford and his team who sell and service trucks. They have their strategy up on the walls in the training room, making it easy to walk the team through it, while operationally they have a whiteboard highlighting key actions out in the workshop where everyone can see it, and it's where they do their daily team huddle. Quarterly Themes are made into posters which are displayed around the facility. Such a great way to keep everyone clear and aligned on what needs to get done.

By clearly and regularly communicating the strategy and related near-term actions in this way, it's easy to monitor progress, the business objectives stay fresh in people's minds, and team members maintain a greater sense of commitment and enthusiasm towards them.

Consider now how you can best communicate your strategy within your own business so that more ethereal and long-term plans are put into action. Depending on your strategy, this internal communication can also be complemented with external communication to your suppliers, partners and customers. Done well, external communications can help both the people within and outside your business to connect to your greater purpose, vision and BHAG.

Keeping the big picture in focus

At all times, the key objective of our communications is to connect the strategy and related priorities back to the foundational principles that we covered earlier in the book: your vision, values and purpose, the aspiration that is reflected in your BHAG and the importance of what you do for your customers. Not only will this ensure there's alignment between your business's beliefs and strategic goals, it will also forge a shared sense of purpose among your employees, which, in turn, fosters a sense of community.

As countless authors and leaders have spoken about before, we humans have a fundamental desire to belong. When you see someone wearing your team's jersey on the way to a football match, you share a bond with them. When you're travelling overseas and you hear someone with the same accent as you, you feel a connection. They are *your* people, because you share something in common with them.

This desire to belong is so strong that we seek it out, through the products we buy, communities we join and businesses we work for. As Simon Sinek writes in *Start with Why*, 'Our desire to feel like we belong is so powerful that we will go to great lengths, do irrational things and often spend money to get that feeling.'[2]

You can assume that your people have this same desire, which raises the question: is your business fulfilling their desire to belong or not? Does it have a sense of community?

As you read in the discussion on purpose earlier in this book, when you clearly communicate what you believe, you will draw in people who believe the same thing, people who will go to

---

2 Simon Sinek, *Start with Why: How Great Leaders Inspire Everyone to Take Action* (New York: Penguin, 2009), 53.

extraordinary lengths to support your business. However, if you stop communicating those beliefs, that sense of belonging fades, along with the desire to go above and beyond to help you achieve your highest goals.

By connecting your strategy, right through to the current quarter's priorities, back to your vision and purpose, you are continually reminding your people of what they are working towards and why. It keeps our heads up at the horizon, rather than down at the weeds.

PROPELLER TIP: As a leader, get better at telling stories that connect values, purpose and strategy. Stories about the founder, your customers and your great team members.

WHEN TO INVITE DEBATE

Even if your strategy is aligned to your business's vision, values and purpose, there will always be those who want to debate it. However, if you've spent weeks or months sending the strategy back and forth, hosting round tables and running town-hall-style meetings, only to see enthusiasm wane when it's time to implement it, you may need to reconsider the timing around the announcement of your strategy.

In a 2012 study on our commitment to goals, social psychologists Gergana Nenkov and Peter Gollwitzer found that when businesses and teams create the opportunity for debate ahead of agreeing to a strategy, although this delivers more rational outcomes, it can plant seeds of doubt early on, which results in *lower* commitment to the strategy.[3] The team ends up suffering from 'strategic planner's remorse'.

---

3 Nick Tasler, 'Get Your Team to Stop Second-Guessing Decisions', *Harvard Business Review*, September 12, 2014. hbr.org/2014/09/get-your-team-to-stop-second-guessing-decisions.

Like the 'buyer's remorse' people experience after a large purchase, strategic planner's remorse is the regret team members feel after buying into a strategy. Essentially, the act of committing emotionally to a strategy creates a sense of great excitement. But when everybody returns to business as usual a few days later, that gives way to remorse. The big difference between buyer's and strategic planner's remorse, however, is that the performance of a purchase won't change based on how we feel after buying it. The performance of a strategy will.

Therefore, if you want to deliver on your strategy, you need to reduce the chance of planner's remorse, and instead create conditions that will foster planner's *resolve*. Fortunately, Nenkov and Gollwitzer found that encouraging debate *after* creating the strategy inclines teams to defend their decision, which then results in *increased* commitment to the strategy. In the strategic planning that I do with clients, the senior leadership team is sent some pre-work to till the mental soil ahead of our formal planning session. Part of that work encourages them to engage their own teams to capture all the important inputs and insights that will help frame the thinking of the senior team. Then, once those top-level decisions are made, the direction and priorities are shared around the organisation, enabling everyone on the team to commit to how they will deliver on their part of it.

To deal with debate when it comes to rolling out the strategy, there are also some techniques that can help. Organisational psychologist Roger Schwarz advocates considering the debate among your employees around a strategy as an adult-grade 'connect-the-dots' puzzle that you need to solve as a group.[4] In a smaller business, this could be facilitated through a detailed seminar with your employees, or in

4 Roger Schwarz, 'How to Break Through Deadlock on Your Team', *Harvard Business Review*, July 7, 2015. https://hbr.org/2015/07/how-to-break-through-deadlock-on-your-team.

a larger organisation it may involve a town-hall-style meeting after which team leaders can come together to discuss the issues raised.

To enable thoughtful resolution of problems, you and your staff need to consider:

- *Assumptions* – what does each contributor to the discussion assume to be true, albeit without evidence?
- *Interests* – what needs are contributors trying to address through their solution or position?
- *Information* – what other relevant data and opinions inform a solution?
- *Connecting the dots* – how can the different contributors form an agreement?
  - Map out the assumptions, interests and information of each party.
  - What pieces do they not agree on?
  - Why did they include or exclude certain items?
  - As a group, decide which items will be considered in developing a solution.
  - Develop the solution as a team.

This structure and transparency enables constructive debate and a collaborative approach that will engender commitment to the agreed solution.

* * *

To sum up, by communicating your strategy clearly and repeatedly, and making sure that it's in alignment with your purpose, values and vision, in service of your clients' core needs, and having a clear, credible and aligned set of priorities, actions and related metrics, you will have built more trust within your business and set the foundations for commitment and accountability which ultimately deliver results. Then the key is to schedule a follow-up session where you invite debate to refine and improve the core ideas and boost commitment, backed by a structured approach to working through any contentious issues.

With this in place we can move on to the critical execution aspects, which are captured in part V: Achieve.

KEY POINTS

1. Solid communication is critical for engaging the whole business in the go-forward plans.
2. Problems arise from a lack of communication, an incomprehensible or misaligned story, and from missing the 'what does this mean for me?' aspects.
3. In the absence of clear, consistent and effective communications, people will form their own version of the story.
4. The key is to align all the elements: what you believe, where you're heading, how you're going to get there, who's accountable for what, and how you'll keep track of progress.
5. Carefully consider timing of announcements and open the type of debate that will drive towards commitment.

TAKE ACTION

Do you think you are ready to communicate your strategy to your people? Consider these points:

1. What is the underlying story that needs to be told from the elements you've built so far?
2. How can you best personally communicate your strategy? Depending on your style and the size of your business, are roundtables possible, an open forum, or a newsletter?
3. What other communication methods can you use to support your messages? What about a podcast or video? (It can't just be one communication element; a combination is required to meet the differing ways that your team will take on information.)

4. What are the most important pieces to share in the initial communications? Remember to focus on how the strategy relates to your purpose, values, vision and customer impact, and how each part of the business will be affected.
5. How could you better capture the insights of your team? When should you invite debate and what must you do to engender full commitment?

PART V

Achieve

'Without action, the world would still be an idea.'

Georges Doriot, Professor, Harvard Business School

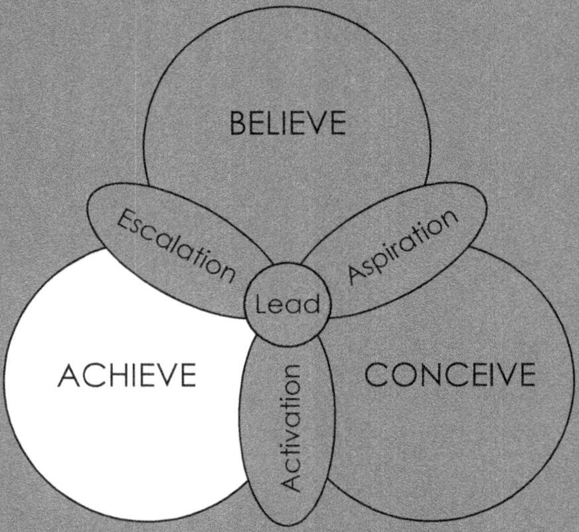

Many businesses make the mistake of creating big plans to achieve big goals, but don't consider the processes, structures and people required to implement them. This results in frustrated staff who are overworked, torn between competing priorities and unable to do their best work; constantly changing strategies to work around resourcing issues; and the financial struggles that flow on from these unending directional changes.

Elements of the **ACHIEVE** sphere avoid those issues by putting in place the pieces you need to implement your strategy effectively – it's about getting clear on what you *do*. Having already considered the emotional and intellectual energy in the preceding two energy spheres, this sphere is about providing physical energy: the bones, muscles and nervous system of your business. This includes enabling the right processes, creating the right organisational structure and populating it with the right people. Once you have these pieces in place, your business will be focused on the activities that are most highly aligned and most profitable, and your people will be empowered to get the most important pieces of work done and done well.

CHAPTER 13

Processes

'Achievement comes to someone when he is able to do great things for himself. Success comes when he empowers followers to do great things with him. Significance comes when he developed leaders to do great things for him, but legacy is created only when a person puts his organisation into the position to do great things without him.'

John C. Maxwell, leadership expert

A COMMON BUSINESS TRAP

Business leaders should strive to create an organisation that isn't entirely dependent on their input – yet so many spend every day intrinsically linked to every action.

Unfortunately, many organisations never overcome this. As a sole trader, owner of a start-up, or leader of a mid-size business you've grown from the ground up, it's often expected that everything will continue to revolve around you. However, even as organisations grow, their teams often lack the clarity and autonomy needed to run effectively on their own, and the organisation remains dependent on its leader. It's a crucial and common constraint.

Does any of this sound familiar?

You get into the office at 8 am to see dozens (or hundreds) of new emails waiting for you, along with messages on your phone and meeting requests. Your team trickle into the office and your morning slips through your fingers as head after head leans around the open door of your office to ask if you have a minute.

Then the meetings start, as you're called on to make 'go' or 'no-go' decisions about a plethora of new ideas and activities. You end political disputes, placate customers who have been rubbed the wrong way, answer questions and take care of the odds and ends that somehow keep getting missed.

Suddenly it's the end of the day and you can finally get back to your own priorities.

Instead, the focus shouldn't be 'the thing' your business does – that is, delivering a specific service or remarkable product – it should be having a *system* that does 'the thing'. I know it can be a tough shift to make. After all, you might be the expert who started your enterprise on the strength of inventing a great product, or the creator of a speciality service that has seen your business become an industry leader. But, as I say to my clients, after years of their business growing, it's now time to move it beyond its teenage phase and into adulthood. And this requires more rigour and discipline (that is, processes and systems) – expectations of adults are different, aren't they?

Fortunately, with the work you've already done on clarifying your organisation's beliefs, aspirations, strategic concepts and activators, you're more than halfway there. The Believe elements from part I of this book have provided the set of permissions for your business, the Aspirations (part II) have defined the performance zone, the Conceive pieces of strategy and risk have created clarity around key thrusts (part III), while the Business Model (chapter 8) gives a sense of how the strategy will be delivered. In part IV, the Activation activities made the priorities clear as well as the expectations about each team's and individual's measurements and deliverables.

Processes are therefore the next piece of the puzzle, as they help us bring all the previous pieces to life. Also, aside from their immediate value to you in running the business now, processes, along with your business model and leadership team, are a key part of any 'business system' that a potential purchaser of your business would wish to buy. So, in terms of bolstering business value, there's good reason to make sure they are thoughtfully set up and operating elegantly.

WHY ARE PROCESSES SO IMPORTANT?

Processes ensure that any regular activities can be taken care of without your input. In fact, organised well, your business should not be reliant on the heroic efforts of yourself or any other individual member of your team. Such efforts aren't scalable or repeatable and, furthermore, they aren't humanly sustainable. The objective is that in any given situation your people will know exactly how to respond and exactly who is in charge of each step in a process. With processes in place, regardless of who needs to complete a piece of work, it will be done the same way every time, resulting in consistent results for both internal and external stakeholders. It's the ideal outcome.

Your refined set of necessary and sufficient processes also reduce clutter by ensuring staff are focusing on what needs to be done, rather than getting lost in superfluous activity.

Sadly, however, especially in fast-moving businesses, there often isn't sufficient thinking about why a process needs to exist and how it should best run. This either results in processes that aren't useable and that eventually get abandoned, or a complete lack of processes as staff tackle situations on an ad-hoc basis.

The other genesis of issues is the freewheeling leader who actually revels in reactivity and leaping into different opportunities so they avoid or disrupt elegant processes (creative entrepreneurs, I'm looking at you!). In case you don't know, this drives your team mad … I know because they tell me.

COMMON PROCESS PROBLEMS

I've found that dysfunctional processes usually evolve over time and generally fall into three categories:

- the 'not necessary'
- the 'inefficient'
- the 'ineffective'.

The 'not necessary' are processes that may be a testament to your business's heritage but no longer serve the strategy. Reporting processes often fall into this category. The risk is that these processes won't readily come to light unless you challenge yourselves to find them, and meanwhile they'll soak up resources that could be better deployed elsewhere. My tip with things like reports is to ask, 'What decision can we make with this?' More generally, we should be testing whether our processes (and the systems that automate them) are providing a better experience for our customers. If they're not supporting better decisions, compliance obligations or delivery, they may be redundant.

'Inefficient' processes either don't make sense or make work unnecessarily hard, which means staff will often try to subvert them. Yes, they may still deliver the right result, but in an inefficient way. These processes may be ones that fail to utilise new technology or don't take advantage of outsourcing opportunities to improve quality, cost and speed. Or, as I've discovered in some client businesses, they may simply be process tasks that were inherited from the previous leader, tipping us into the 'doing it the way it's always been done' category.

These are all processes that could now be better done by someone who's made it a specialty (for instance, supermarkets used to own their distribution function, whereas they tend now to outsource this to specialist logistics companies). Even in my own business, I *could* do all my own social media management, but with all the client-facing coaching, public workshops and speaking engagements I'm doing it will likely fall away, and I won't do it as professionally as Anne, my Content Manager. So we've established a content management process around research, writing, review and publishing that gets the task done.

'Ineffective' processes are those without the right checks and balances to make them worthwhile. For example, having inappropriate sign-off levels for purchases, or inadequate separation of procurement and payables accountabilities. You've invested in the people and systems to deliver a result, and at a superficial level it may look as though you are … until something goes wrong.

Another consideration is missing processes – what should you be doing that you aren't? A related issue is that a business can become so reliant on a specific individual to perform a few tasks that no-one has bothered to really understand and codify what they do. For instance, I've had several clients who had no structured process behind their marketing, but they had grown to a size where it was important to consider. The problem here, of course, is that there will be either risk exposures or missed opportunities from gaps in your process architecture.

By failing to have clear and elegant processes, you disempower your people to make ground-level decisions on a day-to-day basis and complete work to the standard that you, and your clients, expect. This creates problems that the leader wastes time fixing rather than more productive time focusing on the big-picture direction of the business.

Make it a habit to spring clean your processes regularly. Then it's not such a wrench to let them go – it's just part of perennial adaptation.

WHAT PROCESSES DO YOU NEED?

Which activities require processes? Anything that gets repeated!

This may include sales, performance reviews, customer communications (both marketing messages and communications for when things go wrong), collecting product feedback, business continuity planning, payroll processing, training new employees, annual leave requests, working with external providers and more. At a micro level there are hundreds of things to be done, but what you'll find is that most processes can be grouped into these common categories:

- *Employee processes* – these include recruitment, onboarding, learning and development, performance review, reward and recognition and exiting.
- *Product development processes* – these may include processes around sourcing materials, design, production, quality assurance and user acceptance testing, among others.
- *Sales processes* – prospecting and identification, engagement, product or service proposals, commitment and sign-off.
- *Customer service processes* – these include how to respond to enquiries and complaints, how your receptionist answers the phone, regular service scheduling, and more.
- *Finance processes* – these include payroll, accounts receivable and accounts payable, and reporting.
- *Partner and supplier processes* – these might include processes around selecting partners and suppliers, how your working relationship functions, and reviewing the existing relationship.

- *Marketing processes* – these are how you spread the word about your products and services, including online marketing, traditional advertising, events and public relations.
- *Administration and support processes* – these processes might relate to documentation and IT systems, managing projects, strategy development – essentially any of the background work that needs to take place to keep all of the other areas running smoothly.

Take some time to make a list of some of the regular activities in each area which require a documented process. A great way to do this is to map it out visually on butchers' paper or a whiteboard, or use sticky notes for each task so that you can move things around until the picture looks right. I like to get clients thinking about the customer journey of dealing with their business and mapping out the flow of activities from the first touchpoint through to the end-point. You may have heard this referred to as the 'value chain' – how your business creates and delivers value. What you will develop is a jigsaw of intersecting elements from the above list of categories.

In this first cut, my tip is to make sure you accurately map things out as they *are now*, engaging the people who are typically involved. Remember this first exercise is the 'as is' version, not how you hope things work or what the current process manual says. This will be very revealing and you'll undoubtedly get differing points of view among your team of how things work from their own perspectives. Exploring this topic, one of my professional services clients was discussing how they recorded the number of hours they'd worked. Turns out that some parts of the practice recorded all time spent on an assignment, whereas others only recorded up to the billable level of hours that they'd agreed with their client, ignoring the time over-run. This was inconsistent with their policy, created internal incongruence in reporting, and also hid valuable data on what the real cost of delivery had been.

It's great to get insights like this so you can begin thinking about how things could and should be done. It's also especially useful if you ask the question, 'Is that how it happens *every* time?' Invariably, the next level of detail will then start pouring out. You may think, 'Actually, if it's a special order, it happens *this* way', or, 'Dave doesn't like the online ordering system, so he rings his sales orders through.' Keep going until you've developed a clear picture of how your overarching process actually works.

PROPELLER TIP: To check on process rigour, ask, 'How would our best competitor do this?' or, 'How would a business that specialises in this process do it?'

MEASURING SUCCESS

One of the ways to get extra rigour into this piece of the puzzle is to measure process performance. How would you and your team define success at each step along the way? Perhaps it's the number of leads generated by your marketing campaign, the success rate of your new hires, the volume of re-work in your service department, the percentage of A-grade fruit being shipped, the labour efficiency of your team or the value of the sales pipeline. Again, it's whatever the indicators are in your world that tell you the system or process is healthy (and if it's not).

To cut through to the most critical processes that we'd like to measure, I've introduced a number of clients to Jim Collins' 'Flywheel' exercise from *Good to Great*.[1] In essence, this approach is built off an

1 Jim Collins, *Good to Great: Why some companies make the leap... and others don't* (New York: Harper Collins Publishers, 2001), 164.

understanding of what has made your business successful (which you may have captured at a detailed level from the earlier value chain activity), and how each of those success steps has reinforced the steps that follow. Collins drew this out with Jeff Bezos and his team in the early days of Amazon: lower prices on more offerings leads to increased customer visits, which attracts more third-party sellers, which in turn expands the range of offerings and distribution, growing revenue over fixed costs, which enables ... lower prices on more offerings. And around the Flywheel goes again. It becomes a bit clearer where the most impactful processes are, doesn't it? As a cross-check on what you've done so far, what are the systems and processes that really make your business tick? And, importantly, how would you judge the health of each Flywheel step? In that regard, it's ideal if you can determine a prospective and retrospective measure for each. For instance, Amazon could measure both third-party seller enquiries (prospective) and third-party sales or sign-ups (retrospective). They give you a clear indication of what is going on in your process for engaging third-party sellers.

CUTTING BACK

Once you have a sound view of a process, the next step is to remove the complexity and reduce it to the smallest number of necessary steps to achieve the required result.

A good question to ask is: which of your stakeholders (customers, owners or staff) would be willing to pay for this process? It's worth reminding yourself and your team that your stakeholders are already paying for your internal processes: customers pay a premium on your goods or services to fund the process, owners forgo dividend income and staff commit their time. Will each of these groups be happy with the 'spend'?

If not, the next element to consider is whether there are any steps in the process that are unnecessary. Are there any adjustments that would make it better? Are there any people involved who don't need to be? Some people may think that they need to own an entire chain of events, however once a process is defined, it might become clear that if different people owned different parts of the process, it would reduce double-up and make work more efficient. Meanwhile, other steps could be automated or outsourced, potentially making the system better, faster and cheaper.

For instance, it is common for businesses to have a portfolio of projects running, but they often fail to consider what the project governance process is and if it's working. I ran a workshop around this for a retail client's fifteen-person leadership team. They had 140 projects between them with no way they could all be done. Covering an entire wall of their meeting room with butchers' paper divided into a multi-year timeframe, I asked each person to write down their own pieces of the puzzle and categorise them. They were then free to place them on the wall wherever they wanted or needed them to be.

When this was all done, I asked the team to stand back and tell me what they saw. There were a number of key observations. First, that there was too much going on and clearer priorities needed to be made. Second, the weighting of their activities was too heavily skewed towards the next four months, so they decided to reschedule their plans accordingly. Lastly, numerous tasks were misaligned and the dependencies needed to be worked through to make sure that all the pieces of the puzzle were tackled in the required order. Getting a shared view of a process like this can be a very powerful visual exercise, especially when the team builds it together, giving everyone a sense of fairness and ownership in making any required changes.

* * *

As a leader, rather than dealing with all the minor, day-to-day issues and enquiries, clear processes mean you can lift your focus to put more weight behind the big decisions. The team has the information they need to make the day-to-day decisions, which, with robust processes and enabling systems, should run like clockwork, and if on occasion two people or two departments come into conflict about a decision, this is when you come in and decide what is required to achieve your organisation's goals. It becomes the exception rather than the rule.

In other words, these rhythmically running processes help to liberate you as a leader, enabling you to spend less time 'in' the business and more time working 'on' it.

KEY POINTS

1. Your set of processes defines the necessary and sufficient activities that combine to deliver value from your business.
2. Issues arise from poorly conceived, misaligned or redundant processes that stifle effectiveness and unnecessarily drive up costs (and frustration).
3. It is important to review the outcomes expected of your processes against what is happening in practice. Growing businesses will outgrow their processes so they'll need upgrading.
4. Clear processes are simpler for staff, create less system and interpersonal friction, minimise cost and are a key part of your organisation value.
5. Successful businesses keep an eye on the outcomes of processes to monitor their health.

TAKE ACTION

Think of the key processes in your business and consider the following:

1. What is the smallest number of steps required to successfully deliver the major activities in your organisation?
2. Which organisation is your benchmark for your overall system or individual processes? With the rate of change in your industry, how will these processes be done in five years?
3. What must be done internally (perhaps it's part of your core competency or intellectual property), and what could be outsourced? Or stopped?
4. What would you like to measure that is currently a blind spot?
5. How would a new entrant to your industry do this?

CHAPTER 14

Structure

'Every company has two organisational structures:
The formal one is written on the charts; the other is the everyday relationship of the men and women in the organisation.'

Harold Geneen, President of the ITT Corporation

If your BHAG is your destination, your strategy is the direction that will take you there, and your processes represent the most effective and efficient route, your organisational structure is the vehicle.

The problem for most businesses is that their structure was created long before they considered their BHAG and strategy, or it simply evolved over time out of necessity rather than by design. This means that businesses end up with superfluous functions and roles, which can become a political minefield to unpick later, and a breeding ground for ineffectiveness and inefficiency, as well as creating large gaps where the required functions and roles haven't been filled.

It's like building a house without knowing how you want to use it. The architect and builder construct a great house, but when it's time to move in, you discover that it has six bedrooms when you don't have a family yet and just wanted somewhere nice to entertain. Yes, it might be a great house, but it isn't a great house for *you* and your needs.

This is why it's important to design a structure once you know what you want your business to achieve. If you understand where you want to go and how you're going to get there, you can then determine the structure you need to support that ambition. With this focus you can 'organise' your business by determining the key functions or capabilities required, how they will interact to deliver value to your customers, and who should control each piece of the puzzle. You will also establish the idea within your culture that the structure is not a 'rusted on' part of your business – it takes the broader business goals into consideration and it will change as the business's needs change.

By carefully reviewing and redesigning your structure to support the critical processes that you've defined in chapter 13, you create clarity, because every part of your business knows its responsibilities and how it contributes to the big picture. You also avoid creating a culture of empire building where leaders fight over who has the largest department or biggest budget, as everything is based on the goal you want to achieve rather than pointless politics.

Does your own business suffer from any of these issues? It's possible that your business framework was developed when the company was in its infancy, or perhaps it developed without planning as operations expanded. No matter what your situation, this chapter will show you how to hone a structure that supports maximum efficiency and productivity.

GETTING ORGANISED

To begin establishing an effective organisational structure, first grab your value chain – the sequential chunks of activity through which you deliver an outcome for your customer. This takes some of the work you did around process in the previous chapter and takes it a step further. The value chain includes the major sets of activities, processes, functions and related hand-offs that combine to deliver your product or service. Once you have outlined this, then add the support functions that enable your product or service to be delivered – those that support your delivery, but which the customer does not directly see, such as accounting, human resources, information technology and building services.

Second, print out and critically review your existing organisational structure. What are the main functions in your current business? Is the current structure efficient and effective, or are there redundant areas, overlaps or gaps that you've been struggling to fill for some time? Make a note against any areas that may need to be restructured. What approach gives you maximum agility while retaining the unique capabilities that make your business distinctive?

Third, look back at the capabilities you need to implement your strategy. Do they align with your current organisational structure? If not, what are the gaps you need to fill? You might need a larger marketing function, more customer service representatives or more product developers. If your business is growing, you might need more support around human resources, administration or information technology. Perhaps some functions will now be implanted within divisions, departments or regions, rather than being centralised. Make some notes about these areas on your current structure – which existing areas need to grow or change, and what needs to be created?

Fourth, consider the capabilities and functions that might no longer be necessary. To focus on your goals and the strategy to achieve them, ensuring that the entire business is aligned, you will need to cut back on anything that doesn't support it. Perhaps there are aspects of the business that relate to discontinued products or services that either need to be redirected or closed down. Or, if you want to expand into a new region with your existing product suite, you may not need a function for developing new products. By contrast, if you want to remain in your niche but develop a revolutionary product, you may not need separate regional teams or offices. Again, mark the areas that are no longer necessary.

For those capabilities that you do need, do you already have them in-house? If not, can you grow them, purchase them as services or acquire them (either by buying a business or a team)? Or are they one-off or short-run requirements that, on a cost/benefit basis, it's not worth creating an in-house function for?

One of the mistakes businesses make at this stage is getting focused on the people. They start to think, 'We couldn't make a change here, because that might leave Jess out of a job.' This is dangerous – it can prevent you making the changes required to deliver your ultimate success.

Instead, just focus on the required functions for the moment, and in the following chapter on people I'll discuss finding and keeping the right people. If someone's role is no longer necessary but their strengths and values are a great match for your business, there's no reason why you can't move them to another part of the business and focus on building their capability in that new area.

Finally, consider the relationships between the different functions you require. Which areas could be combined for efficiency and effectiveness? In smaller businesses, sales, marketing and customer service are often combined and many of the roles have responsibilities in all three areas, which enables constant communication between them. However, if your business is growing, it might be time to split these areas and ensure that each role is clear, to create a more streamlined customer experience.

With each of these considerations in mind – your value chain, current structure, required capabilities, redundant functions and relationships – sketch out a new organisational structure. You may need to try a couple of versions and work with your leadership team to get this right, but as long as your desired organisational outcomes are the focus, you will be on the right track.

PROPELLER TIP: The structure you had as a start-up will need to be evolved to enable growth.

FILLING YOUR STRUCTURE WITH THE RIGHT ROLES

Within the major areas of your organisational structure, you will need to establish the roles required to carry out various functions and processes.

This is another area I find many businesses get wrong. Typically, clear roles and accountabilities are not defined, which results in no-one taking ownership of the various functions and processes and the results they are expected to achieve. Unsurprisingly, results flounder. Additionally, the rest of the business doesn't know who is responsible for what, which means there's nowhere to turn when something goes wrong, and also no-one to take charge when you want to implement something new. The result is interpersonal friction, wasted time and missed opportunities.

So, when reviewing your organisational chart, consider the key responsibilities of each of the major functions. What are the major outcomes they need to deliver and key tasks they need to carry out? Who are the stakeholders with which that area engages, and what are the measurable results you expect them to achieve?

Make a list of each of these responsibilities, checking in with the leader of each area to ensure you have the correct understanding. At this stage, don't worry about the individual roles – simply list the responsibilities for each function. For example, if you were reviewing the marketing department, you would simply list every responsibility in that area, rather than figuring out what the marketing assistant does versus the social media guru versus the graphic designers.

When you are listing the responsibilities, focus on the responsibilities required for delivering your strategy, rather than an area's *current* responsibilities. If you only look at current responsibilities, you may start listing tasks that are no longer required, given your new objectives, or defining the role according to the way the current incumbent has operated. However, if you are future-focused on those aspects required for your strategic success, it will be much easier to ensure each role is accountable for contributing to strategic outcomes.

Next, categorise these responsibilities. Depending on the area, this may be by seniority (to continue the marketing example, this might be administrative tasks performed by the marketing assistant, versus strategic plans made by the marketing manager), by area of expertise (so in marketing this might be public relations, customer communications, traditional advertising and online marketing), or there might be another method of categorisation that is more relevant to your business.

Then review these groups of responsibilities. Is each group large enough to comprise a full-time role? Would some smaller groups be more appropriately filled by a part-time or casual employee? Do some larger groups need to be covered by two people? Are there roles that could be combined, such as administration assistants for different teams, which may improve communication across the business? Again, this is something you may need to confirm with your leadership team, who will have different and possibly greater insights into each part of the business.

Once you have confirmed these roles, you can then add them to your organisational chart and write relevant position descriptions. These position descriptions should cover:

- the key responsibilities and delegations of authority
- how this role contributes to the business's strategy
- the key performance indicators the employee is required to meet, and how these contribute to the strategy
- the competencies required for success in the role
- key relationships this role has with other roles and areas of the business.

In my client cohort, I typically encourage them to create Topgrading Scorecards for each role, based on the *Topgrading*[1] book by Bradford Smart. These scorecards allow leaders to make better decisions about the resources and staffing required to support their business structure, assess role fit and performance and thereby achieve strategic goals.

This objective approach proved instructive for one of my clients, an allied health provider serving the aged-care market. The leadership team had concerns about the performance of an interstate clinic, so I got them thinking about a scorecard for the clinic leader role. As they talked through the expected outcomes and success metrics of the role, the accountabilities and the competencies required, they realised that the person they'd appointed did not measure up. The rigour of the scorecard approach gave them the confidence to transition the current manager out, as they realised the gaps were unassailable and provided a much more robust picture of what to seek in the next appointee.

1 Bradford Smart, *Topgrading*, 3rd edition (New York: Penguin Group, 2012).

MAKING THE CHANGE

No matter how established your current business structure may be, if it doesn't take your medium-term strategy, process set, BHAG or vision into consideration, it will fail to serve your objectives.

In some cases, major changes may not be needed – you might just need to change the focus of the existing teams in your business so they are delivering against your strategy. For other businesses, a complete overhaul may be required. While this will involve making difficult decisions, it's a necessary step towards achieving your goals.

Once you have your organisational structure and know the roles you need to fill it, the next step is deciding on the people who will fill these roles. It's important not to get 'stuck' here. Unfortunately, in my experience, there are often temptations to keep people in roles for the wrong reasons: politics, history, family, a sense of guilt for a former poor hire, avoidance of conflict, and more.

Keeping people in a sub-optimal structure in the wrong roles and for the wrong reasons will *not* take you closer to delivering your organisation's potential. In fact, it will mean all the work you've done so far – defining your purpose, values, vision, BHAG, customer expectations, strategy, business model, and the key activation enablers – will be hamstrung in delivery.

What you have done through the preceding chapters has built a rational case for the structure you're adopting. To follow through on executing your strategy within the ideal structure, you now need to look at your people.

KEY POINTS

1. Structure is the vehicle, or organisational bones, that will help you reach your destination.
2. Beware the risks of history, politics or loyalty that keep you operating in a sub-optimal structure.
3. Structure must be determined *after* you know where you are going strategically and have defined the core processes and functions required to get you there.
4. Follow the steps. Assess your value chain, existing structure and the capabilities you need or could remove.
5. Once the core functions are established, define the key roles required, along with the accountabilities, reporting lines, metrics and communication channels that connect them all.

TAKE ACTION

There is a lot of work to do in this section – have you followed the steps? Once you have, ask yourself these questions:

1. If you were starting a similar business today, what structure would you adopt?
2. To what extent, in your current structure, do you have individuals who can be readily held to account for the performance of your functions and processes?
3. Based on the way you need to mobilise to deliver on your promise to customers, does your organisational structure need to change?
4. To understand motivations, who has something to lose if you changed your structure today? How would their behaviour manifest?

5. What changes could you start to make to improve the structural cohesion of your business? For instance, are there unnecessary hand-offs, slow points, interpersonal friction or gaps in the way you operate now?

CHAPTER 15

People

'Great vision without great people is irrelevant.'

Jim Collins, business author

At the start of the Australian football season, every team is already assessing the strength of their bench. For teams that failed to secure a place in the previous year's Grand Final, their coaches, boards and playing groups will all be hunting down ways to secure that all-important trophy in September.

As a Collingwood fan, I was interested in reactions to the club's choice not to renew contracts for several star players shortly after their last triumph; especially those players who were a vital part of Collingwood's last premiership win. While these contract cessations are often disappointing for supporters, they are sometimes a necessary evil in building future capability. In these instances, Collingwood's coaches stepped up and made the hard decisions, selecting their list by addressing one key consideration: retaining and developing the players capable of playing in the *next* premiership.

Your business's team is just as critical. Your focus should be finding and developing the people who will help you win your own premiership, just like it is for the coach of an elite sports team.

These are the people who don't just keep your customers and colleagues satisfied, they turn them into raving fans who will spread the word about your business. What's more, these employees are likely to continue to work with you in future. These people will empower your business to adapt to the changing industry, economic and technological landscape surrounding it. These are the valuable people who keep your day-to-day processes running, the strategic priorities delivered, and contribute to living the values and purpose so that 'business as usual' is just that.

Furthermore, in a world where industries, economies and technologies are developing at an increasingly speedy rate, businesses need to readily evolve if they want to survive. But they can't evolve with the wrong people who remain attached to the way things were, lack cultural alignment and decrease productivity. The best and brightest people will help your business adapt to a changing landscape, and can even drive change for the better through contributions to strategy, a new product development idea, promotions initiatives or remarkable marketing materials and, most importantly, contribute to shaping and strengthening your culture. In short, they bring the energy you need to power the way forward.

FREEDOM TO FOCUS ON THE BIG PICTURE

When you find and invest in the right people, the leaders in your business are able to focus on the bigger picture. The wrong people are high maintenance – they need micromanaging, motivating and someone to clean up any messes they leave in their wake.

The right people, on the other hand, can comfortably do their work in alignment with a business's values and purpose, are attracted by the gravitational pull of your vision, shared aspirations and the strategy to deliver it, have the strengths and capability required to excel in their role, and can independently make the decisions expected of someone at their level. With this level of philosophical alignment, capability, self-motivation and self-direction, it also means that less bureaucracy is required to manage them.

As business author Jim Collins wrote in *Good to Great*, 'The right people don't need to be tightly managed or fired up; they will be self-motivated by the inner drive to produce the best results and to be part of creating something great.'[1]

One example of a business whose success has been underpinned by a focus on attracting and retaining the best people is Nucor, the largest steel producer in America. The company believes that if people perform well in their roles, they should be rewarded with generous bonuses and guaranteed job security. In fact, the business has not laid off a single employee since it began in 1967, even during economic dips. This culture has resulted in consistently high productivity and impressive employee loyalty. With the right hardworking, productive people in place, the company's senior management can then focus on their greater vision and maintaining Nucor's position as an industry leader.

Nucor is testament to the fact that if the people on the 'frontline' of a business are reliable and committed, it enables senior leaders to concentrate on the big picture.

WHAT IS THE MISSING PIECE IN MOST BUSINESSES?

Despite the many benefits of having a productive, self-reliant workforce who attract lifelong customers, most businesses fail to develop a talent strategy. People strategists at Bersin by Deloitte found that

1 Jim Collins, *Good to Great: Why some companies make the leap... and others don't* (New York: Harper Collins Publishers, 2001), 42.

only twelve per cent of their 454 *Global 2000* organisation survey respondents have a rigorous talent strategy to hire the right people.[2]

Most businesses focus on hiring people based on their competencies and experience, rather than choosing people who, in the first instance, are a values match and share the bigger vision. This results in disconnected staff who don't bring their full energy and talent to the business; your leadership team's time being consumed with the niggling issues that accompany these misfits, such as mopping up relationship issues and fixing mistakes; and high attrition rates, with the wasted time, cost and energy that ensues.

Furthermore, when it comes to the right people already on board, many businesses don't use them correctly once they are hired. In his book *Go Put Your Strengths to Work*, Marcus Buckingham writes that only seventeen per cent of employees play to their strengths 'most of the time', while employees in high-performance teams play to their strengths seventy-five per cent of the time.[3] It's tough to compete with that differential if it's working against you. If you don't know the strengths of your people, they can end up in the wrong job, which means that not only are they frustrated and unfulfilled, but they aren't performing as well as someone else might. As a business, then, you aren't getting the results you could be getting from that role, and you might even be paying for extra roles to pick up the slack. Additionally, if the person's strengths aren't being used, the business is also missing out on the results that person could achieve in the right position. This is hard for the individual, hard for their boss, and hard for the business.

---

2 'Bersin by Deloitte: Clear Talent Strategy Linked to Better Business Outcomes', *Bersin by Deloitte*, April 29, 2015, bersin.com/News/Content.aspx?id=18473.

3 Marcus Buckingham, *Go Put Your Strengths to Work: 6 Powerful Steps to Achieve Outstanding Performance* (New York: Free Press, 2007).

Meanwhile, other businesses have the right people in the right job, but haven't put the effort into developing the person so that they can achieve what's required in the role. Again, this leads to the business not getting the best value from the role, and leaves the team member feeling frustrated and more likely to search for fulfilment elsewhere.

Career management firm Right Management conducted a study that found seventy-nine per cent of businesses have no strategic workforce plan to ensure they have the talent they need in the future.[4] This is despite thirty-six per cent of businesses reporting a lack of key talent in key positions, and eighteen per cent reporting a shortage at all levels, despite most companies claiming people are their most valuable resource!

Ultimately, these common mistakes create ineffective teams comprising indifferent, bored or scared team members. Ideas are dismissed, ridiculed or ignored. Arguments are frequent, and often unresolved. Deadlines are missed because team members are disengaged or incapable in their role, and therefore unproductive. There is a lack of clarity around individual roles and responsibilities, and team members neither trust nor help one another. This then impacts the way they treat your customers, and it's a slippery slope from there.

THE 'DREAM TEAM'

An effective team is usually made up of a wide variety of personalities and capabilities, each of whom contributes in a different way, complementing one another's strengths and weaknesses. If you imagine a team comprised solely of planners, it would not be able to cope with ever-changing deadlines, while a team comprised

---

4 'Too Few Organizations Have Confidence in Leadership Pipeline', *Right Management*, July 10, 2014.

only of high-level, big-picture thinkers might never get organised to deliver an outcome. Think of your favourite sports team – they are very clear about what they require in each role and always strive to pull together a balance of players with the right mix of skills to win the day… goal-kickers, defenders, the speedy and agile, the heavy and strong.

In the ideal business team, the members feel like a valued part of the broader company and get personal satisfaction from their contribution. The team environment is supportive, which means the members feel secure enough to take risks, be innovative and communicate their honest opinions. This also means the team is comfortable with friendly, professional conflict, and is able to easily resolve disagreements without pandering to individual egos. Decisions are made on a 'best for business' basis.

An effective team has clear objectives and priorities (but only a critical few). Every team member understands those priorities and objectives and is fully committed and accountable to achieving them, and they understand how their individual objectives fit into the broader business objectives. This should all be clear from your work on the Activation section.

Team members have clearly articulated roles and responsibilities – which you mapped out in the previous chapter – and all other team members are fully aware of those roles and responsibilities. In the spirit of being a team, they also support and help one another to deliver on their responsibilities.

As the business and the team grow, the team learns from, and builds on, previous projects and jobs, implementing improvements and innovations. Accordingly, they don't suffer the debilitating malaise of most businesses that perpetuate their mistakes.

THE TRAITS OF A-PLAYERS

Building a great team starts with finding the right individuals, which comes down to two criteria: whether or not they are a values match for your business, and whether or not they have the capability you need to deliver on your strategies through success in their role.

Ideally you want people to be both a strong values match and a strong capability fit. I call these 'A-players', drawing on the work of Geoff Smart and Randy Street in their book *Who*.[5] However, if you need to choose one or the other, it's best to choose someone who possesses the right values, with the potential to grow into the capabilities you need. This concept is true for any business that achieves greatness.

Take, for instance, the online shoe retailer Zappos, a company renowned for its highly collaborative workplace culture and outstanding customer service. To them, the 'right' people aren't chosen based on capability. In fact, their website doesn't even post vacant positions. For Zappos, the focus is on getting to know the potential hire, rather than trying to slot them into an available position. As they say on their website, 'We want to get to know you, whether there's a current opening or not! We wanna hear from you, chat with you and learn more about you … and job postings kinda get in the way of that!'

Instead, they focus on people who are a match for Zappos's ten values, some of which include delivering 'wow' through service, creating fun and a little weirdness, pursuing growth and learning, being passionate and determined, and being humble.

Throughout the interview process, Zappos determines whether or not a candidate is a values match. When a candidate is from out of town, for example, the company will pick them up from the

---

5 Geoff Smart and Randy Street, *Who* (Ballantine Books, 2008).

airport in a Zappos shuttle. At the end of the day, the interviewer will ask the shuttle driver how the candidate treated them. Zappos CEO Tony Hsieh says, 'It doesn't matter how well the day of interviews went, if our shuttle driver wasn't treated well, then we won't hire that person.'

If the candidate is offered the job, during the training process Zappos then offers them $2000 and a week's salary to quit. Those who'd rather take up the financial offer than the role are not considered a values match, and will not be considered for another position with Zappos in the future.

These hiring practices have resulted in a highly engaged workforce that is famed for employees who go above and beyond when it comes to customer service, which has proved a key feature in the company's success.

While not all businesses will undertake such drastic measures as Zappos, the company is testament to the importance of always measuring new hires or existing employees against your list of values. Understanding the current mix of values and capability has been one of the most critical insights that my client leadership teams have had, highlighting the underlying cause of friction, weak performance and overwhelm for leaders.

Remember, capabilities can be taught. Values can't.

PROPELLER TIP: Map your team on a grid to understand where everyone sits with regard to values alignment (vertical axis) and productivity (horizontal axis).

BUILDING CAPABILITY

In his *Harvard Business Review* article titled '21st Century Talent Spotting', Claudio Fernández-Aráoz, senior adviser at the global executive search firm Egon Zehnder and the author of *It's Not the How or the What but the Who*, describes a situation where he was asked to find a new CEO for a family-owned electronics retailer that wanted to expand.[6] Working closely with the outgoing CEO and board, they created a shortlist of the relevant competencies for the role, which they used as a basis for screening candidates. Their final choice had all the right credentials, experience and competencies, however he was unable to adjust to the significant changes occurring in the market at the time, and was asked to leave after three years of poor performance.

By contrast, at the start of his executive search career, Fernández-Aráoz was asked to fill a project manager role at a small brewery owned by Quinsa, a company that dominated the beer market in southern Latin America at the time. Unable to identify a pool of people with the right industry and functional background, he contacted Pedro Algorta, who he'd met in 1981 when they were both studying at Stanford University. Algorta had no consumer goods experience, he had never worked in sales, and he was unfamiliar with the province in which the brewery was located. However, Fernández-Aráoz knew he had the potential to grow into the role and recommended him to Quinsa. The applicant was appointed, quickly promoted to general manager, and eventually became CEO of Quinsa's flagship Quilmes brewery. The story demonstrates that if someone is a values match for your business, you should look at them very carefully. A person does not necessarily need to tick all the boxes from the get-go – their capability can be developed, whether through on-the-job training, formal education or coaching.

---

6 'The Big Idea: 21st-Century Talent Spotting', *Harvard Business Review*, June 2014.

WHAT DO YOU DO WITH PEOPLE WHO ARE NO LONGER A MATCH?

Obviously, not all of your people will be with you for the entire journey. In fact, as your business evolves at an increasing pace, you may end up with even greater churn. After all, not everyone is going to be a match for your business, and those who can't be developed will need to be exited or re-assigned in the structure if their skills and values are a match but they can't go up a level. For instance, you may have had a bookkeeper in the early days of your business, but they are unlikely to have the CFO-level skills such as dealing with bank covenants or leading an acquisition that you may need as you grow. However, if their financial skills are sound, you might still have a role for them elsewhere in the finance function.

But for those who do need to go, there are three sorts of exits. The first group includes those who are exited for transgressing your values. The second group includes those who don't have, and haven't been able to develop, the capabilities required for the next steps in your business. The final group are those whose role is no longer required due to a structural change.

In a business that has strong values, a values breach is generally a very clear-cut conversation.

When your values are clear, an employee who breaches one needs to go. If your values haven't been clear until now, you can have a conversation about your values and give them a warning, but if they breach them again they need to be exited, albeit in alignment with all the relevant employment law. Remember, as the leader of your business, your decisions have the most impact on whether or not that business lives by its values. The people you choose to keep and let go are a key way to demonstrate your adherence to the cultural norms that you established in part II of the book.

In a former job, I heard of a colleague who hadn't been given what she considered to be a 'deserved' salary increase. In response, she started flying herself interstate and going out with her friends on the company credit card. When the company discovered her behaviour, she was asked to leave, because it was against their values. No one blinked – it was clearly the right decision.

PROPELLER TIP: As you consider your ambitious multi-year goals, be deliberate about the fit and calibre of the team you'll need to get there.

When it comes to those who don't have the capabilities required for the next steps in your business, assuming they're a values match, exiting should always be the last resort. Instead, focus on the other options for them. Can they be coached? Is there some other area where that individual's skills and strengths can be still used in the business – a different function, a project that leverages their strengths?

The key thing to keep in mind is there are some cases when the journey of the business will exceed the journey of the individual. If they can't grow with the business, then it's time to consider a graceful exit. This is a far better alternative than creating a role for the sake of keeping someone in the business. First of all, they know that the job's been created for them, which can make it destructive to their self-esteem. Second, it doesn't send a great message to the rest of the business. Instead, the person should be able to leave with dignity and, where possible, your support in finding another role.

The key to a graceful exit is acknowledging the work that the individual has done to date. While they may have helped you achieve your current level of success, the business is facing a massive challenge, and their skills would be put to better use elsewhere.

In fact, often these folks will say to themselves, 'This is a great time in the strategic journey of the business to get somebody who can really take them on that next race. I loved my time here, but now it's time pass to the baton to someone else.'

But don't we value our people?

Businesses, and the people within them, often struggle with exits. The reason is many businesses genuinely value their people and appreciate the role they've had in helping them get to where they are today.

In this context, Jim Collins makes an interesting distinction in his book *Good to Great* between the idea of being rigorous rather than ruthless. Ruthless businesses, he argues, focus on hacking and cutting in difficult times, often firing people without consideration. Rigorous businesses, on the other hand, consistently apply exacting standards at all times and at all levels.[7]

Collins found that companies that made the transition from good to great were rigorous, not ruthless. This principle applies to all stages of people management.

When you are hiring, you need to rigorously apply standards to the candidates you select. They *must* be a values match. If they are not a values match, you need to keep looking until you find the right person, rather than thinking the wrong one will be 'good enough'. Ideally they will also have the capabilities your business needs to grow to the next level. If not, they must be able to develop those capabilities. Remember in these considerations to distinguish between those capabilities and attributes that are learnable and easy to learn versus those that learnable yet hard to learn. And be

7 Jim Collins, *Good to Great: Why some companies make the leap… and others don't* (New York: Harper Collins Publishers, 2001).

particularly aware of innate traits such as work ethic. Attributes such as this I don't see as learnable, so they need to be spotted early.

Then, when the team are on board and you are developing your employees, you need to ensure everyone who has the desire to grow has the same opportunities to develop. When you require someone to develop new capabilities, they need to have access to the same coaching experiences as everyone else and be evaluated by the same standards.

As the business moves forward and you believe you need to make a change to your team, you must act. When you suspect a values breach, the process must be the same for every employee, from the initial investigation through to potentially suspending the employee, conducting a formal investigation and either exiting or reinstating the employee based on the outcome. When someone is not performing at the level you require, you must give them the opportunity to build their capability or move into another role (assuming, of course, that they are a values match).

One final attitude of rigorous companies is that there is no such thing as a redundant *person*. The *function* may no longer be required by the business, or that *role* may no longer need to be performed, but the human being is not, and should never feel, redundant.

* * *

Taking control of the people aspects of your business is, in my experience, one of the most fundamental leadership capabilities as it so strongly influences success in all the other aspects of your business. Amongst my clients, their ability to get an A-team on deck has been a key performance differentiator. Through *Scaling Up* we learned that a cohesive talent strategy that puts the best people in the right jobs will foster a more productive, self-reliant workforce, freeing up time for business leaders to focus on the bigger picture. Furthermore, when a workforce feels they are part of a strong, vibrant and fair system, their satisfaction and commitment will be reflected in the work they do and the results they achieve.

KEY POINTS

1. Having the right people in the right roles in your business is critical to its success.
2. There are frequently gaps in values match or capability that lie unaddressed and cause friction and underperformance.
3. Your business beliefs should inform the philosophical match of your people, while your strategy and priorities will guide your sense of the capabilities they require.
4. Alignment of beliefs and abilities will be achieved through how you recruit, develop and exit staff.
5. You need to be constantly vigilant on team health and capability, especially in fast-growth businesses.

TAKE ACTION

Getting the right people 'on the bus' is a fundamental leadership requirement, so consider the following:

1. Review the people in your business. Who are the A-player performers – those who are both a strong values match and have high capability?
2. Who are the high-potential employees – those who have strong values, but whose capability needs to be developed?
3. How can you best develop your high-potential employees' capability?
4. Where are the risks – those who are not a values and capability match and who could damage your business? Create an exit plan for these individuals.

5. Based on your existing team and the capabilities you require, do you need to consider bringing in more talent? Is it a new role, or a new person in a current role?

PART VI

Escalation

'Every success story is a tale of constant adaption, revision and change.'

Richard Branson

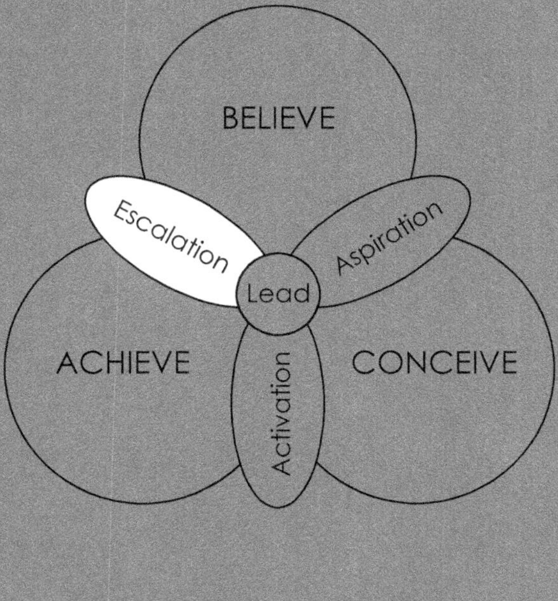

ESCALATION connects the *Achieve* actions taken by your business and people to what you *Believe*. Reflection on success and failure allows you to extract important learnings to guide your business for its next upward spiral. Rejoicing in the achievements through Celebration puts energy back into your team and reinforces those beliefs, which ensures they continue to inform business decisions. The Reset is about framing the next iteration of the propeller. The more things continue to go right with organisational performance, the more positive reinforcement goes through the business as a strong, growing and vibrant entity, the more valuable the business becomes, and the easier it is to lead. You avoid getting stalled.

CHAPTER 16
Reflection

'Success is not final, failure is not fatal;
it is the courage to continue that counts.'

Winston Churchill

REFLECTING ON YOUR SUCCESSES (AND FAILURES)

In the *Harvard Business Review* article 'Why Leaders Don't Learn from Success', Francesca Gino and Gary Pisano argue that businesses use models, theories and principles to guide their actions and decisions.[1] Using your successes and failures as tools for learning empowers you to update these models, theories and principles, and to make better decisions in future.

The ability to learn from success and failure is apparent in every business that has grown sustainably. Apple's success with the iPod and lack of success with its predecessor personal device, the Apple Newton, informed the company's theories behind what makes a successful product. Virgin's success in air travel but failures in bridal wear, cosmetics and cola provided valuable lessons about the markets where Virgin would be more likely to experience success.

1 Francesca Gino and Gary Pisano, 'Why Leaders Don't Learn from Success', *Harvard Business Review*, April 2011, hbr.org/2011/04/why-leaders-dont-learn-from-success.

Likewise, reflecting on your annual and ninety-day strategies teaches you how to improve your results so you can ultimately deliver your medium-term strategies. In measuring his business's ninety-day achievements, one of my clients found that in the course of six months, his team was delivering on eighty per cent of the commitments they made to each other, they recorded their best revenue month ever, their largest ever sale, and had far outperformed their profit budget.

On the flipside, though, without reflection, your business will be vulnerable to repeating the same mistakes.

Most businesses see success and failure as the result of their efforts. I see success and failure as learning tools. Failure in particular creates an opportunity to avoid previous mistakes and do better in the future. Which isn't to deny that it can't be a bruising experience. Business, like many other competitive areas of life, is a confidence game, and the honest reflections that failure requires from leaders and those around them can lead to some serious second-guessing. However, the ability to have this introspection and to then internalise the lessons learnt is a hallmark of strong leadership. My approach with clients is to undertake reflective exercises formally every quarter. This has two benefits: it normalises having a review of what is working and not working, and it brings up any issues more quickly. It's always far less painful to deal with early-stage problems than to let them grow.

LESSONS FROM SUCCESS

Few businesses consciously reflect on their successes. Success is commonly viewed as evidence that your strategy and practices work, which can then lead to overconfidence in your knowledge and capabilities.

However, without reflecting on your success your business runs the risk of becoming complacent. By assuming that success is a sign that everything is going well internally, you ignore the external factors that may have contributed to your success. This can also lead you to assume that *everything* is running smoothly when, in fact, one part of your business might be carrying the rest of it.

By reflecting on your successes, you can address these issues as well as learn how to transfer the skills and assets that contributed to your current success to the next project or industry. This teaches you how to recognise opportunities and leverage resources and gives you a foundation on which you can build.

So when you experience a success, ask your people:

- What contributed to this success? Consider both internal and external factors.
- Why did these factors have such an impact? Use the five whys exercise, which I covered in the Purpose chapter, to investigate the root cause of the success.
- Can these factors be replicated? And, based on the level of success, the potential time and expense of replication, and any shifts in trends, is it worth trying to replicate these factors?

This introspection can be difficult (remember the old adage 'success has many fathers, but failure is an orphan'). However, many learnings come out of this process, making it one of the keys to escalating to new levels of success.

LESSONS FROM FAILURE

Arguably, because of the emotional connection to the associated pain, most of us learn far more from our failures than our successes. Failure teaches you what your business isn't good at. It signals when a strategy is off key, which process would be best to outsource, or where partnerships would be more valuable than trying to own a particular area yourself. It creates an opportunity to redirect your focus so you can concentrate on where you get the biggest bang for your buck. It also signals that you may have veered from your core beliefs. At least it does if you pay attention to it.

So where do you start? When it comes to failure, Harvard Business School Novartis Professor of Leadership and Management Amy Edmondson[2] says that there are three types of failure:

- *Preventable failures* – these may include deviations from processes, values breaches, or oversights due to unclear accountabilities.
- *Unavoidable failures* – due to the uncertainty of your business's work you encountered an incident that you hadn't dealt with before and failed to manage it effectively.
- *Intelligent failures* – these failures are a result of experimentation, testing and trial and error.

The learning to be gained from each of these failures is different.

In the case of preventable failures, the aim is to figure out the weak link in the process or activity and rectify it so the same failure can be avoided in future. If it's a procedural failure, you would revisit the process, as described in the Processes chapter. If the failure was a result of a values breach it would, depending upon severity, trigger a range of responses from supervisor feedback through to instant dismissal, and a reminder to be more stringent around values-based recruitment in future. If the failure was due to someone's responsibilities being unclear, you would need to revisit your structure and the accountabilities of each role to ensure everything is covered.

---

2 Amy C. Edmondson, 'Strategies for Learning from Failure', *Harvard Business Review*, April 1, 2011. hbr.org/2011/04/strategies-for-learning-from-failure.

When it comes to failures that were unavoidable, the question is whether or not you can make that failure avoidable in future through addressing processes, structure, people and strategy. Can you tighten your risk management approach? Was there a change in trend that was missed? Do we need more data points to give a better picture of our market context?

When it comes to intelligent failures, these are an essential part of growing your business. The key here isn't avoiding them, but creating a safe place for experimentation to occur. One of my personal learnings from trading the financial markets many years ago is that failure and loss is an inherent part of the game as there are no certainties. So smart traders get clear on their beliefs, build an aligned strategy, execute the plan and manage the risks. It's really no different in business, except that leaders tend to have a less developed appetite for admitting they are wrong, and therefore don't look for the evidence.

In contrast, let's consider McDonald's, which has been challenged by changing customer wants, an increase in competition and downward price pressure over the last few years. As a result, the fast food giant's financials have been suffering and they are taking strategic action in response.[3] This includes trying new concepts, such as building your own burger, trimming promotional offerings, and tackling new markets such as selling its coffee in grocery outlets. While some of these experiments may fail, if they have considered the risks beforehand and safeguarded against possible financial losses, they can safely test new ideas. What's more, by reflecting on the new products that fail, they can learn what to avoid in the future and channel their efforts into experiments that have succeeded.

3 Stephanie Strom, 'McDonald's Modifies Business Strategy as Sales, Earnings Drop', *Smart Investor*, January 25, 2015. smartinvestor.business-standard.com/pf/Pfnews-290447-Pfnewsdet-McDonalds_modifies_business_strategy_as_sales_earnings_drop.htm#.Vd1LF_mqqko.

Detecting failures

Regardless of the type of failure, you want to create a business culture where you can detect failures quickly, and people feel they can safely report them. Your people need to understand the types of failures to expect as well as why openness is essential to solving them and helping your business grow. Keeping this in mind, those who *are* open about failures should be recognised for coming forward, as this creates a safe environment for other employees to start reporting.

In most cases, failure should be a learning experience, rather than an opportunity to apportion blame. The only incidents worthy of blame are values breaches and failing to deliver on your own agreed accountabilities. If you've been successful in establishing your performance culture, you shouldn't be dealing with these incidents. If they do come up, your responsibility as a leader is to have clear standards so you can address them quickly.

When a failure is reported, the next step is analysing why it occurred. Again, the five whys exercise is an invaluable tool for finding the root cause of any failure, which then gives you the information you need to categorise the failure and put measures in place to avoid a similar incident in future.

The final activity to effectively learn from failure is to have a system for strategically producing intelligent failures. While reflecting after failing to achieve a long-term BHAG has some value, it's far more valuable to have a lot of small failures leading up to your eventual achievement so you can learn, innovate, and apply course corrections as you go. Some examples include launching a beta program to a small segment of your market for feedback, user acceptance testing, or working with focus groups on product ideas and marketing campaigns. As I write this, one of my clients is trialling a low-cost version of their service through a simple online system that they had built in 42 days and is being project managed by a tight team of three with a small sample of their client base. Low risk, small investment, quick review. In my view, more businesses should be running product and service experiments as part of their growth and renewal.

By building experimentation into your strategy, you can fail quickly on a small scale and use this information to escalate as you go, rather than failing on a scale large enough to jeopardise your business.

KEY POINTS

1. Reflection is a crucial part of the learning journey for leaders, as an opportunity to appraise both failure and success.
2. Success shouldn't be met with complacency – there is always room for improvement and there is great value in leveraging wins.
3. There are three types of failures: preventable, unavoidable and intelligent. Each one needs to be approached differently.
4. Unless there has been a values breach in your business, failure provides a positive opportunity to learn, rather than to simply apportion blame.
5. Having analysed performance, put measures in place to amplify successes and avoid repeating the same mistakes.

TAKE ACTION

In reflecting on your own business, consider these questions:

1. Do you have the mechanisms in place to learn from your successes and failures?
2. How do you communicate them?
3. How would you describe your appetite for failure? What impact does that have on your team and business?
4. What needs to change to enable more intelligent failures?
5. Given your learnings, what are some course corrections that you should be considering right now?

CHAPTER 17

Celebration

'Celebrate what you want to see more of.'

Tom Peters

TAKING A MOMENT

Earlier in the book we looked at the importance of taking away lessons from your business's successes. However, another aspect that is sometimes overlooked is the importance of taking the time to actively celebrate your company's achievements too.

My client Damien told me straight up, 'As entrepreneurs we're terrible at celebrating'. Other clients have since agreed. The reason: a high level of drive and expectation can mean that these leaders are never satisfied as there is always something yet to be achieved. While the ambition that sits behind this is useful, in my view it has a longer-term detrimental impact on organisational energy and is therefore not sustainable.

Doing it well, on the other hand, brings great energy. An early highlight of my career at consulting company SMS was the celebration of the London office opening. The invitation was on a specially made CD that had been crafted into the shape of a British bowler hat.

The tables at the event were decorated in a British theme and a large number of staff had spent weeks rehearsing for the annual company pantomime, which involved numerous themed songs. With a large contingent of consultants and their partners present, everybody was engaging in the spirit of the event and the atmosphere was electric.

On the whole, though, I don't reckon that businesses celebrate enough. And with the really big goals they're chasing, especially those that will take years to be fully realised, it's too long to wait if they only celebrate success at the end.

This is especially true for Type-A entrepreneurs who are on a perpetual growth path, always moving onward and upward to the next battleground – there's a tendency to fail to stop and recognise the smaller victories along the way. But leaders actually need to make time in the shadows of their business's latest achievement to pause and recognise and appreciate those who made it happen. This is a great opportunity for you to connect the team back to your purpose, vision, strategies and the execution elements that made it all possible. This not only energises the next undertaking, but it also creates a little gap for the positives and the learnings that you've captured to be shared.

A failure to celebrate success and honour efforts can foster a culture of dissatisfaction in which people only focus on the shortfall between the business's current state and its ultimate goal, rather than feeling a sense of pride and motivation based on the progress they've made so far. Take, for instance, my high-growth clients who typically aim to increase their business by fifty to one hundred per cent in the medium term – while these goals are important and stimulating, there's also a risk of frustration about how daunting the objectives may seem. A dissatisfied team may get caught in a negativity spiral whereby they purely focus on what they *don't* have, while a satisfied team that celebrates their achievements is better placed to face reality and build upon what they *do* have.

As the leader, this sets you up to work with your team to do simple things to stay aligned, such as setting the quarterly priorities, accountabilities and measures we looked at in the Activation section of this book. So make sure you honour commitment and effort, support your team with a positive 'how can I help?' attitude and enjoy the growth process. Remember, getting to your ultimate business goal is a marathon, not a sprint, so take the time to rejuvenate and give thanks where it's due.

'How important it is for us to recognise and celebrate our heroes and she-roes!'

Maya Angelou

MAKING IT FUN

So how else could you acknowledge your business and employee achievements? One way is to make a game of work. The rise of electronic games in entertainment has segued into workplaces, with a new trend of 'gamification'. Gal Rimon from gamification company GamEffective argues that while managers are closely engaged with the strategy, goals and related KPI and performance process, those in the non-managerial ranks have simple targets or quotas. They accordingly have less engagement in the process, and Rimon reckons this can be positively overcome with gamification. The games, which can be easily played on mobile devices, for instance, drive alignment with corporate strategy, but their narratives lend them a fun feel with scoreboards and events to track and celebrate progress. Could you gamify anything at your work? It can be especially useful to get results shared through technology as your team gets larger and more dispersed, providing a technological means of capturing and recognising success and keeping everyone connected. But don't let this get in the way of the principle here: share the story about the progress and wins. Frankly I'm a strong fan of the low-tech solutions, such as whiteboards: easy, cheap and quick to implement, simple to update, and readily visible. And don't be afraid to mix the mediums. At Ecotech there is a large honour board in the foyer recognising long-serving staff, they've installed TV screens around the office with a scrolling presentation on latest results, and in the boardroom we capture quarterly highlights on butcher's paper.

PROPELLER TIP: Use the highlights you've collected through the month to storytell at company town hall meetings, in your newsletter and on social media.

MAKING IT REGULAR

When I'm working with client leadership teams, the first agenda item at their Quarterly Review is to list the highlights. They are frequently surprised, even as the most senior leaders who have the best overview of what is going on within their business, at how much they have achieved. Often, in the flurry of their demanding daily operations, these successes have gone unnoticed. So I pick them up for a couple of reasons: first, to create and share a sense of progress and success; second, to generate some energy in the leadership team to start the day; and third, to capture the individual successes so that they can be used in communications by the leaders. Because our businesses aren't like a sporting contest where the result is known within a couple of hours, we need to be deliberate about installing moments of celebration at milestones along the way.

* * *

Of course, there are many ways to celebrate achievements. It can be as simple as highlighting successes within an internal newsletter to your staff, or as elaborate as a formal gala event, such as the one I enjoyed at SMS Consulting. It's also important to consider what it is you celebrate. Sure, it's great to recognise sales and revenue targets being met, but what are some broader measures of success that can be acknowledged? It could be related to your quarterly strategies, the completion of a particularly challenging project, actions that have demonstrated the strength of your values and purpose or tied in with any charitable work that your organisation is involved in.

Most clients have adopted a regular rhythm, either monthly or quarterly, to get their team together for a town hall meeting where they share the success of the most recent period. In addition, it's a great leadership touch to make a moment to celebrate right when things happen. For instance, my client Gaethan Cutri uses his WhatsApp channel to send personal video messages to Cutri Fruit staff spread out across his orchard business, thanking everyone at the conclusion of a successful harvest. James Agius at Ecotech holds regular company-wide huddles where the latest updates are shared in a combined live and virtual format. Meanwhile, over at UCS, Stephen Ellich has been reinforcing their brand promise by onsite visits to each crew that delivers a first-time pass on their projects (which is almost one hundred per cent of them).

Like these leaders, you'll find that rejoicing in victories throughout your business will boost morale, engagement and energy in your team, which will be positively reflected in the work that they do.

KEY POINTS

1. Because business is an ongoing venture, we need to be deliberate about making moments to celebrate.
2. There is a tendency to under-celebrate, or to just celebrate public events such as Christmas or the end of the financial year, which may be uncorrelated with the timing or nature of your successes.
3. Rather than just celebrating financial results, it's important to celebrate success in all its forms.
4. Celebrations are more powerful when anticipated, so set up the important ones well in advance and watch the energy build.
5. Celebrations don't need to be big, expensive parties. Small and regular moments are very effective too.

TAKE ACTION

Think about how success is recognised in your own business and consider these questions:

1. What is going on right now in your business that might be an opportunity to celebrate?
2. Are current celebrations just around financial results, such as hitting an annual profit target, or are there some wider markers of success that you could leverage?
3. What is an objective in the medium term for which a celebration could be promoted and the whole team could look forward to and work towards together?

4. What about very short-term celebrations? What could you do for hitting a weekly, monthly or quarterly objective? What about when you complete a large project or when new staff are inducted? Or when you achieve a target level of charitable contribution?
5. How can you easily keep this culture going without it becoming a drag? Are there some people within your team who could share the duties around?

CHAPTER 18

Reset

'Knowledge comes by taking things apart: analysis. But wisdom comes by putting things together.'

Dr John Morrison, American politician

TAKING STOCK

Maybe your business is close to a major 'BHAG-like' milestone, or perhaps it has already past the first big goal you set. This is a great opportunity to reinvigorate the business for the next phase of the march towards fulfilling your Vision and living your Purpose.

Great businesses have a notable ability to achieve their BHAGs. After all – this is how they became great.

The US and NASA landed a man on the moon within ten years of the BHAG being announced. Walmart exceeded its 1990 BHAG (when it had US$25 billion revenue) to become a US$125 billion company by the year 2000. And Red Balloon reached its fifteen-year BHAG to reach ten per cent of the Australian population in nine years.

However, what keeps them great is the ability to replace an achieved milestone with a new one. This is the final element that enables great businesses to escalate from success to success, whereas businesses that suffer from the 'We've made it' syndrome can quickly plateau, or even go backwards.

To return to NASA, it suffered from this syndrome after the successful moon landings. Ford became complacent after success in democratising the automobile. Microsoft lost its way after putting a computer on (almost) every desk.

So, whether you're at a major milestone that you've achieved over a decade, whether you're reviewing your three-year strategic progress, or whether you're taking stock at the end of a financial year or end of quarter, the lifecycle stage may be different but the principle is that same: relative to my goal, where have I got to?

FINDING THE NEXT BHAG

Our lofty goal only drives a business when it hasn't been achieved. Once it has, it's all too easy to lose momentum, and the only way to get it back is to find the next one – something that is just as big, hairy and audacious as the one you created ten or fifteen years ago.

In that regard, we can take a lesson from Tesla boss Elon Musk. To progress the company's BHAG of widespread adoption of electric cars, he announced that Tesla was going open source with its technology intellectual property.[1] This has two drivers, one stated and the other not: Musk notes that a key part of Tesla's purpose is accelerating sustainable transport, so using patents to block technology access for competitors actually works against their own ambition. The other driver is that, without allowing critical mass to develop in the electric car market, the enabling infrastructure ecosystem would be slow to emerge. Accordingly, freeing up the patents helps Tesla achieve its vision and carry out its strategy. It has also been good PR

1 Elon Musk, 'All Our Patent Are Belong To You', Tesla Blog, June 12, 2014. tesla.com/en_GB/blog/all-our-patent-are-belong-you.

and Musk believes that their technology leadership will help him attract top engineering talent.

This is the final secret to avoiding a growth or performance stall – finding the next BHAG. And for those still working on their first one, its about finding the next set of medium-term objectives that keep you tracking even closer to your big vision, embodying your values, and empowering you to live your purpose.

I quite like the analogy of an expedition or a hike or a march. We've come quite a way and we're taking a breather before tackling the next hill.

So, as we use this moment to reset, what is the next hefty objective that marks this part of your business journey?

WHAT'S IN THE WAY (NOW)?

Back in chapter 7 when we were crafting the Strategy, I asked you to reflect on, 'What's in the way?' Now that we have done a circuit of the propeller approach, having addressed those early friction points, it's timely to get clarity on what is *now* in the way as you consider the next part of the climb.

You're at a different vantage point now and, armed with the Reflections you've collected along the way, you'll likely have insights on some new and different challenges that are either present right now or will emerge as you walk this next part of the trail. To get my clients thinking this through, I tend to ask things like, 'What would a company twice your size be doing?' I also like them to bring in feedback from staff and customers, and to interpret the challenges that we identify – is there a pattern emerging from these data points?

WHAT MUST BE DONE?

With an insight into where we're headed as a business, the learnings we've absorbed and the blockers that have been surfaced, we now have some more decisions to make.

For some of my clients this has meant a refresh of some senior roles, others have needed to mature their systems and processes, for a couple of them it has represented a moment for the founder/owner to hand over the reins to a professional external CEO, while for several it has been a time to get much more capable at marketing. In a couple of cases it has also been an appropriate time to exit, passing the baton to a strategic buyer for the next phase of the journey.

PROPELLER TIP: Book in a regular cadence of review with your senior leadership team to track progress and make adjustments.

The cadence of these resets will depend upon the speed at which you're moving and how dynamic the context is where you're playing. As Verne Harnish says, 'the faster you're growing the faster you need to pulse'.

As a guide, I recommend that my clients adopt a model like this from *Scaling Up* for doing periodic resets with their senior leadership team:

- *Annually* – set/revise multi-year capability developments (we usually have a three-year view) and the related initiatives for the coming financial year.
- *Quarterly* – set ninety-day priorities and make course corrections against the annual plan.
- *Monthly* – make course corrections against the quarterly plan.

- *Weekly* – task-level adjustments regarding commitments for the month.
- *Daily* – huddle to check in with what's next and discover any 'stucks'.

Think about this like a sports team: they huddle during mini-breaks while the game is in progress so that they can fine-tune the current game plan. When the game is done they have a weekly review to refine their game plan ahead of the next contest (check on the statistics, what's working/not working; how each of the players are going in their role). As the season rolls through, the considerations become more strategic (are they going to make the finals or do they start shaping the team and approach for the following year?).

Again, this is another element that contributes to energy in your business – a fast, regular beat to your leadership resets will help you scale.

KEY POINTS

1. A business that remains true to its beliefs, vision and values has a solid foundation to expand and branch out into new directions.
2. Success shouldn't be met with complacency – there is always room for improvement.
3. Many businesses, though, lose their edge once a major goal has been achieved.
4. Part of your role as a leader is to identify the next BHAG or multi-year objective.
5. That next growth opportunity might be through quite a different model.

TAKE ACTION

Things to consider as part of your reset:

1. Once you achieve your current BHAG, what might the next one be?
2. As you've gone through the Propelling model, what insights have you had that will inform what you do next?
3. Who will you need to be to drive this next escalation of the business? A bolder leader, more of a visionary, a deal maker? Or will you exit?
4. How do you feel about your business now? How strong and robust does it feel?
5. As you reflect on the spheres and blades, which parts of the model are in need of more help to enable the next lift?

PART VII

Leadership

'If your actions inspire others to dream more, learn more, do more and become more, you are a leader.'

John Quincy Adams, statesman and diplomat

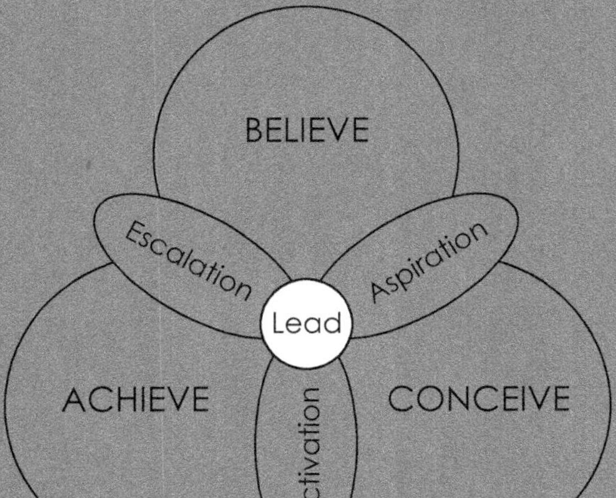

In this final piece of the Propelling Performance model, you need to focus on your own role leading the business. In fact, **LEADERSHIP** is the critical spindle that drives the propeller. As the leader, your job is to ensure that the blades keep turning and that all the energy spheres are congruent and connected.

This role as the spindle means the leaders help guide how fast the propellor goes and the power and energy it generates. This then dictates the altitude to which your business ascends, and the trajectory and rate at which you climb. Leaders drive the process of turning ethereal beliefs into sensible, tangible strategic choices which can then be executed. Without strong leaders who make things happen, all of the other pieces in the model remain theory, rather than practice, and your business will struggle to adapt and grow. To get it right, we need to lead on three levels: leading ourselves, leading the team and leading the business.

CHAPTER 19

Leading yourself

'When I dare to be powerful, to use my strength in the service of my vision, then it becomes less and less important whether I am afraid.'

Audre Lorde, civil rights activist

An essential quality that strong leaders share is a deep understanding of themselves. In the same way that you understand your business's purpose, values and vision, you need to understand your own.

However, many leaders don't spend time looking inward because they are so busy trying to achieve external results. Instead of focusing on their inner purpose, values and vision, they get drawn into the urgency of this week's operational performance, the monthly financial results, and issues with clients and staff. This insight was reinforced by Bill George, the author of *Authentic Leadership: Rediscovering the Secrets to Creating Lasting Value*, who noted that these external successes typically aren't sustainable without the internal foundation of self-awareness.[1]

1 Bill George, *Authentic Leadership: Rediscovering the Secrets to Creating Lasting Value* (San Francisco: Jossey-Bass, 2003).

So why are you in this business? What do you hope to achieve in your life? What sort of person do you want to be? And are those beliefs congruent with the core beliefs of your business?

For your business to be congruent with its purpose, values and vision, the people within the business need to act in alignment with those ideals. Actions must be based on its values. Decisions must be made in service of its vision. And everything must be fuelled by its purpose.

This starts with you, especially if you are the most senior leader, founder or significant member in a family-owned business.

If you are the one at the centre of the propeller, the leader who has the power to make it spin faster and bring together all three of the 'spheres' I have described, then you must do this through your own authenticity.

Leadership coach Kathleen Taylor-Gadsby, writing for the Forbes Coaches Council, suggests that we tend to get dragged into dealing with the 'what' of our roles, whereas great leadership stems from leading from our true selves.[2] Consider these questions:

- What gets you up in the morning? What is your source of motivation?
- What are you great at? What talents and strengths invigorate you?
- What beliefs and values guide your life? How congruent do they feel with those of your business?

Reflecting on these points, how would you rate the connectivity between your own purpose, values and vision and those of your business? Or between your own strengths and what is expected of you in the business? Consider what is standing in the way. What could you do to bring them closer together?

2 Kathleen Taylor-Gadsby, 'What Are The Secrets To Great Leadership?', *Forbes*, July 17, 2017.

When these factors align, you will feel a deeper connection to your role, have greater clarity about the direction of your business and feel more energised to achieve results.

PROPELLER TIP: Set aside some time alone each week where you can think and reflect. You may find additional insight through meditation or journalling.

Remember, the leader of a business has the greatest impact on whether the business as a whole embodies its values. As a result, for you to bring your business to new levels of success, it *must* be in alignment with your authentic self.

It's only when you as a leader are congruent with the business as a whole that you will start to build momentum through the energy and focus you bring to it. Incongruence removed, the business will start to buzz through its aligned belief system. People will be excited to be involved in your business. Those aligned employees will take their place as leaders, and will be your most fervent supporters as your business performs and grows.

THE THREE TYPES OF PROFESSIONALS

While a successful leader must align their belief system with that of their business, they must also have a clear understanding of where their professional strengths lie. Business author Michael Gerber describes the three types of people within any business in his classic book *The E-Myth*. These are the Technician, the Manager and the Entrepreneur.[3]

---

3 Michael Gerber, *The E-Myth Revisited: Why most small businesses don't work and what to do about it.*

Technicians are functional experts. They live in the present, focusing on the work that needs to be done today, knowing that the more work they do, the more money they make. The Technician's comfort zone is determined by how much they can do themselves.

Managers, on the other hand, are the organisers. They are pragmatic in nature and are good at organising people and processes, and their focus is on achieving results through the Technicians they manage. Managers are the ones who turn a business's vision into tactical information that will achieve that end goal.

Finally, Entrepreneurs are the visionaries. They focus on guiding the business towards a greater vision and engaging Managers in that vision.

When it comes to your organisational structure, people who are predominantly Technicians are the ones who carry out the work. They deliver the services, develop products, answer customer enquiries, and provide administrative support. Managers are the bridge between the Technicians and the Entrepreneurs. They lead teams, manage the workflow, clean up messes and keep all processes running smoothly so the Technicians can focus on their work.

An Entrepreneur brings the ability to set the path for a business, to seize opportunity from the changing landscape surrounding the business, to enrol staff in their mission, and to attract the right people to a business. They bring alignment so that people understand, '*That*'s why we're here!' And they translate the purpose, values and vision into strategy.

However, many of the people who launch and lead businesses aren't naturally Entrepreneurs. They are typically Technicians who have suffered what Gerber calls an 'entrepreneurial seizure' and decided to start a business based on their skillset. For instance a plumber thinks, 'I like plumbing. I should buy another five vans and have another few people and start running a plumbing business.'

Likewise, the accountant sets up an accounting firm, the lawyer sets up a legal firm, the baker sets up a bakery and the graphic designer starts offering design services.

But while they might be a very good plumber, accountant, lawyer, baker or designer, they might not have the ability to lead, engage, hire, fire, design or run a great business. In other words, these Technicians often don't have the skills and mindset of the Manager or Entrepreneur, which can hold their business back.

They need the traits of a Manager for efficiency and effectiveness. The skills of the Entrepreneur shape where a business is heading, and they use this vision to guide the decisions they make today. Meanwhile, a Technician is only focused on the job at hand. This is what keeps many small businesses small – their leaders can't get past the functional level.

On a practical level, if you're a Technician, you're on the right path now as that type of focus has likely helped you to succeed in developing and delivering your products and services to a satisfied cluster of customers. That's a great foundation and a lot of my clients have come to me because they've been Technicians who've grown a solid business and now want to really scale it. I trust that this book is helping to illuminate and enact the different roles that need to be played in taking your business forward.

PLAYING TO YOUR STRENGTHS

Of course, even after aligning your beliefs with those of your business and developing your inner Entrepreneur, you may still find that there are areas in which you struggle as a leader. It's important to be upfront with yourself about these weaknesses, and consider whether you need to delegate certain parts of your role.

One of my clients was a technology company founded by an engineer. It is a couple of decades old and is in the top handful of business in the country in its niche, and the founder was interested in listing the business. Now, he is an inspiring leader and an excellent engineer who is core to the technology the business develops – however, he lacked the knowledge and experience to make the necessary executive decisions to list the business on the stock market. While there was a bookkeeper who had successfully handled the finances up to that point, it was also out of their realm of expertise to see the business through the listing.

After careful deliberation, he decided to create a role for a senior financial executive to deal with the markets during the listing and to oversee the financial arm of the business into the future. This allowed the founder to focus on his areas of expertise and prevent mishandling of a crucial function within the business. He knew himself and the needs of the business well enough, and to his great credit was humble enough, to make a very sound decision.

This type of situation is a common challenge for the leaders that I coach. Frequently they have founded the business on the basis of their core technical skill (as an engineer, surveyor, lawyer, accountant, physio, designer – the list is of course endless) and a dose of entrepreneurial spirit. Accordingly, it's very easy and appealing for them to get pulled back to their foundations. My client Nicholas freely admits that this is him: he is a strong engineer, he enjoys diving in to help the team and, frankly, he is sometimes happier with the immediate enjoyment from resolving an engineering issue than working on a longer-term strategic challenge. I still remember him smiling as his engineering leaders told him to stop attending the weekly technical review meetings. On one hand an obviously proud moment that he'd built a capable team that no longer needed his technical input, but also a certain sense of loss as his own role evolved more strategically.

While your team may, like the team at Ecotech, be grateful for the short-term assistance, what the business really needs is for each of us as senior leaders to lift up, as Nicholas has done, and lead at a higher level. In their case it has now been taken to yet another level, with his 2ic James becoming the new, and very capable, Managing Director.

Now, consider where your own strengths lie. What part of your role do you channel your greatest strength and passion as an expert and a leader into? Are there parts of your role that are better off performed by somebody else so that you can put maximum focus into delivering the strategy of your business? If so, you may need to finetune your structure to delegate responsibility to somebody else within the business or create a new role to ensure that certain executive-level duties are carried out by someone with the requisite expertise and experience, freeing you up to concentrate on what you do best. My client Damien did this at Dimple. With the increasing growth and complexity of his business, he showed great humility to bring in an external CEO, Nick Beckett, who had proven experience in leading fast-growth firms. This freed Damien to spend more time playing to his strengths as an entrepreneur and being the founding face of Dimple's vision and values to staff and customers, whilst Nick drove strategy and operations. The combination of their skills and the calibre of the team that they built was a key factor in the accelerating performance of the business and the success of their sale process.

The main takeaway from this chapter is getting really clear on your own role in the business and where you'd like it to evolve, which sets you up for how you'll lead your executive team.

KEY POINTS

1. By aligning your own purpose, values and vision with those of your business, you will feel greater commitment to the business's objectives.
2. Within any business there are Technicians who carry out work based on their expertise, Entrepreneurs who set the path for a business and drive innovation, and Managers who act as a bridge between them.
3. Many businesses get stuck because the founder/owner/senior leader has not developed sufficient breadth around these roles that is required for success.
4. If there are areas where you can't develop capability as a leader (or don't want to), you may need to delegate responsibility to somebody with the necessary knowledge and experience to undertake them.
5. When you lead with authenticity, clarity, confidence and alignment you will inspire commitment from those around you.

TAKE ACTION

Thinking about your personal leadership:

1. How well do you know and own your beliefs?
2. Based on your strengths and interests, what is your best role in the business?
3. How will you continue to grow yourself at a rate that exceeds the growth of your company? What are some of the

gaps between where you are now and where you need to be to become a great leader for your team?

4. What is your personal legacy?
5. What standards do you hold as a leader? How does this measure against what you expect of others?

CHAPTER 20

Leading the team

'No-one works for you, they all work with you.'

Peter Nankervis (aka Dad)

Having a deep understanding of your people is crucial to building a high-growth business. Why? It builds trust.

According to Patrick Lencioni's *The Five Dysfunctions of a Team*, there are five key causes of dysfunction in any team, and the baseline issue is an absence of trust.[1] The others are:

- fear of conflict
- lack of commitment
- avoidance of accountability
- inattention to results.

When there is an absence of trust, the team won't be genuinely open with each other and this leads to infighting, personal empire building and a lack of cohesive action towards a united vision. This lack of trust leads to a fear of conflict, which festers so that teams

1 Patrick Lencioni, *The Five Dysfunctions of a Team: A Leadership Fable* (San Francisco: Jossey-Bass, 2002).

can't have rigorous and productive debates. The inability to debate opinions then leads to a lack of commitment within the team, followed by an avoidance of accountability. Not surprisingly, these four dysfunctions result in an inattention to results, where a lack of accountability leads to personal goals and egos trumping the collective goals of the team.

These learnings are vital, as you can only be successful growing a business if you leverage the contributions of a great team.

This fact was brought into focus by authors Geoff Smart and Randy Street when they interviewed hundreds of successful leaders for their book *Who*.[2] These leaders attributed the foundations of their business success as follows:

- Fifty-two per cent was attributed to managing talent.
- Twenty per cent was attributed to execution.
- Seventeen per cent was attributed to strategy.
- The remaining eleven per cent was attributed to external factors.

Looking at these statistics, it's clear that no matter how well defined your BHAG, strategy, processes, roles and structure are, without the ability to effectively manage your team, success will likely remain elusive.

BUILDING TRUST

'To lead people, walk beside them.'

Lao Tzu, ancient philosopher

The first essential step to managing talent effectively is building trust within the team, as it's only when there is a stable foundation of

2 Geoff Smart and Randy Street, *Who: The A Method for Hiring* (New York: Ballantine Books, 2008).

trust that the team can overcome any other dysfunctions and ultimately achieve their goals.

I've found the best way to start building trust is simply by understanding your people.

Make a commitment to learning about your people's personal histories. Where do they come from? What was their childhood like? Do they have families? What are they passionate about? What experiences shaped them?

There are a lot of important things that happen in people's lives that fashion who they become. These impact their self-reliance, resilience, their levels of trust of others, their sense of independence, and much more.

A person's life experiences inform their behaviours. Yet most of the people leading businesses have no idea what's happening in their employees' lives outside of work. This not only means that they're losing the opportunity to build trust and a deeper relationship with these employees, it also means they're missing out on opportunities to leverage traits and behaviours that could serve the business in achieving its vision. Even those who haven't had what we would consider to be major life-changing events have had experiences that have moulded who they are. Ask them about their first job, or their worst job, or any study they may have done. In my coaching practice I tend to run this as a leadership team exercise over dinner during their annual offsite – there are always deep and remarkable stories that come out, important insights that leaders learn about each other and, importantly, newfound respect from the deeper understanding that they now have of their colleagues.

Finding out what's *really* going on

My dad worked in the transport, logistics and warehousing industry, which is a very fine-margin industry so there is no room for superfluous costs. During the 1970s, the business he worked for was taken over by a UK company, and at one stage they sent one of the UK executives to go through the books to figure out the profitability right down to *every truck* in the company.

Dad managed dozens of trucks, and the UK executive approached him about one of his drivers, Henry. The executive said, 'Henry's truck isn't making money. You need to sack him.' To them, the company was just a set of numbers. Dad refused, which took the executive by surprise. 'I've just given you a direct instruction,' he said, 'You're going to sack him.'

Again, Dad refused. He said, 'Maybe you didn't hear me. I'm not going to be sacking him. Henry is supporting three children and his wife has been battling cancer. Yes, he sometimes knocks off early and he doesn't get his last run done on the truck. But he knocks off early so he can go home and get the kids dinner. So, he's not going to be sacked. End of discussion.'

That night my dad came home and said to my mum, 'I might have just wrapped the job up, but I'm not going to sack Henry.'

Now imagine Henry's position. Yes, he was having a difficult time at home, but his job was secure and he could provide for his family. He knew his boss understood his personal circumstances and was willing to be flexible. He was able to trust his employer to support him.

In the long run, Henry remained a dedicated, valuable employee and Dad went on to foster a large and loyal cadre of staff for whom he genuinely cared, and in return he received 'above and beyond' efforts when it really counted. As a testament to the longevity of these workplace relationships, he and mum recently went to the funeral of a former mechanic, Pierre, with whom he had *stopped* working thirty years ago. Mum and Dad knew it was still important to go along and support Pierre's wife Margaret (see, even I know their names because he talked about his team so often) and their family.

'Western business people often don't get the importance of establishing human relationships.'

Daniel Goleman, psychologist and science journalist

Understanding your people

Understanding your people gives you the opportunity to support them at a far deeper level than you could have otherwise, and this means they are more likely to support you and your business in return.

This starts as trust between you and your people, which flows on to a higher level of trust between the people within your business. And once you have this trust, you'll find that the other dysfunctions within your team are far easier to unravel.

I mentioned earlier that a leader needs to create commitment to their business's journey. If we return to Lencioni's five dysfunctions, you'll see that this commitment can't be achieved in a team that has a fear of conflict, and healthy debates can't occur in a team that lacks trust. Instead, teams with an absence of trust try to preserve what Lencioni refers to as 'artificial harmony'.

Once a team has trust, however, it becomes safe for them to engage in rigorous debates about approaches or ideas suggested by other team members. This debate then allows team members to fully commit to a course of action – those who were in favour of the approach are able to further convince themselves, those who were on the fence are able to see the merits of the approach, and even those who were opposed tend to buy in because the debate allows their point of view to be discussed (and remember, this isn't about degenerating into pugilism or personal attacks, it's collaborating to surface, understand and resolve a problem) . Once they are committed, team members become accountable, and this leads to the team achieving its collective goals.

And it all starts with understanding your people. Of course, this is not instantaneous – the building of trust and the ability to have constructive debate and conflict takes time. For those who can achieve it though, it represents a huge performance multiplier.

PROPELLER TIP: Gradually build your organisational muscle by practising acts of trust, conflict, making commitments and holding each other accountable.

A DRIVE FOR RESULTS

A leader can't simply be a terrific, angelic human being who always gets on with the team. At the end of the day, you are running a business to serve your clients' needs and provide your team's livelihood. This means you need to manage both the people and the performance side of the equation. To do this, you need a drive for results.

Let's now concentrate on these two important elements: 'drive' and 'results'.

Drive

Drive is something that Jim Collins describes in *Good to Great* as 'unwavering resolve'. He writes that 'leaders are fanatically driven, infected with an incurable need to produce *results*.'[3]

---

3 Jim Collins, *Good to Great: Why some companies make the leap... and others don't* (New York: Harper Collins Publishers, 2001), 30.

This drive is essential to achieve fast growth, as it underpins everything that has been discussed so far. Drive is what keeps a leader focused on the business's purpose, vision, BHAG and strategy ... and delivering on the promise to their customers. Drive is what forces them to uphold values, even when doing so may lead to difficult decisions.

This trend is evident in every great business, and every great leader. Every great leader has had to make difficult decisions. When Steve Jobs returned to Apple in 1997, he quickly cut the majority of the company's products. CEO of Whitbread Alan Parker sold the Marriott Hotel chain he had built from the ground up so he could focus on the company's two core growth businesses, Premier Inn and Costa Coffee.

None of these decisions were easy. But they were made because each of these leaders was driven by a focus on the bigger game.

Sometimes this can seem at odds with wanting to support your people. However, what's interesting is that a leader with this drive, a leader who is unwilling to compromise on what's required to make a business great, who is authentic and has built a congruent business as we've discussed in this book, is the one who attracts likeminded people as the business grows.

Results

The next element is 'results'. If you are running a business, your responsibility is to deliver results. This is your responsibility to your staff, your customers, your shareholders, your suppliers and, ultimately, your vision and purpose.

People gain more fulfilment from businesses that are seen as high performers. Customers are more likely to buy from them. Other businesses want to partner with them. Investors want to buy into them. However, in order to experience this, you need to perform.

And this comes down to both understanding what good results are and having a drive to improve them.

Understanding your results comes back to being clear on your customers and business model, which I discussed in part II, Aspiration and part III, Conceive. Who are your customers? How do you reach and relate to them? What is your value proposition? What are your revenue streams and cost structures? What are your key resources, partners and activities? How is success being measured across all its dimensions?

Improving your results comes down to having a deep understanding of which strategic levers can be pulled to achieve optimisation, an unwavering focus on your business's beliefs, and attracting and developing a group of top performers who want to go on that journey with you. It's in this regard that we need to go beyond leading our immediate team and consider how we lead the whole organisation.

KEY POINTS

1. Understanding the people in your business builds trust, which allows teams to discuss challenges honestly and openly.
2. Healthy discourse and debate is essential to creating the commitment and accountability among your people that will deliver results.
3. Many businesses will lack the strength and will to build a fully functional team, and they appear complacent or weak.
4. Leaders should be driven by results, even though this may sometimes involve making unpopular decisions.
5. High-performing businesses with strong beliefs and an eye on results will ultimately attract the right people.

TAKE ACTION

Think about how you lead your own team and reflect on these points:

1. How can you get to know the people you work with on a more personal level?
2. What else could you do to foster a culture of trust among your team?
3. How can you ensure that your team feel comfortable to honestly and openly discuss issues and challenges within the business?
4. What tools and techniques could you use to encourage people to work with an eye on team goals rather than individual performance?
5. How can you help your direct reports to cascade their leadership?

CHAPTER 21

Leading the business

'Great leaders are almost always great simplifiers, who can cut through argument, debate and doubt to offer a solution everybody can understand.'

General Colin Powell, former US Secretary of State

Leadership is the glue that holds a business together. It is the element that underpins all the other areas covered in this book. Without strong organisational leadership your purpose, values and vision end up being a marketing device rather than living elements that drive your business. Your strategy may look good on paper, but it won't get implemented. And even though you may have an organisational structure, processes and roles mapped out, these rely on having the right people to fill those roles, carry out those processes and deliver the outcomes. Accordingly, we need to keep leading at a higher level.

MAGNIFYING YOUR IMPACT ACROSS THE WHOLE BUSINESS

So now, having developed our self-leadership and enhanced how we lead our direct team, it's time to consider how we can magnify our impact across the whole business. This has three key elements:

- being clear about the journey

- staying consistent and aligned with the fundamentals
- telling stories.

Let's take a look at each of these.

Being clear about the journey

Is a change in perspective all that is required for effective leadership?

I don't think so. I feel there's more to the puzzle than simply a shift in mindset. If you consider the role of the leader, while embodying the vision, values and purpose of a business is essential, there is more to it than that. This isn't just a spiritual or philosophical task.

As I discussed earlier, a leader needs to be able to engage others on the business's journey. If the people in your business, your partners and your customers aren't also living your business's purpose, values and vision, then they aren't living qualities of your business. You want the people involved in your business to be passionate advocates for what you believe – this sense that they've joined a cause, rather than simply doing a job.

Then, having connected their heart into the business, you get greater access to their mind. As we covered in the Conceive section, we need our team's best thinking to drive the intellectual energy in the business, so we can agree 'how' we'll be more unique and valuable.

Those strategies then need to be delivered, so as we move into the Achieve section we're committing to 'what' needs to be done and 'who' will do it. Executing against our plans and getting the results, albeit with likely bumps along the way, feeds back in as evidence of living our beliefs.

Again, the energy that we've created in each section is a valuable input for all other parts of our healthy organisation.

This sense of the journey is the most crucial part of leadership – holding up the goal, illuminating the path to get there and the aligned behaviours and actions you'll take to stay on track ... and enrolling others as you go.

This is always one of my highlights as a Coach, when I see great leaders shining and businesses building momentum through an ever-increasing number of their team getting on board. Stephen Ellich has done this well as Managing Director of UCS Group where, from the very start of our engagement, he wanted every leader to be part of the strategic process. This entailed a group of close to forty leaders ranging from the founder and private equity investors, to the senior leadership team and operational crew leaders. Whilst it's not a trivial exercise to have such a large group involved each quarter, there has been a substantial payoff in terms of clarity, alignment and the resulting performance of the business.

Ross Gallagher has similarly multiplied his leadership at aged care provider IRT. Starting with his own senior leadership team in the Home Care division to get the core parts of the model nutted out, Ross was soon getting me involved to help cascade these principles down the next layer to his operational leadership team and also up a layer to the Group Executive. And again, the results speak to the value of clarity and alignment across a business.

'Peak performers want more than merely to win the next game. They see all the way to the championship. They have a long-range goal that inspires commitment and action.'

Charles Garfield, psychology professor, University of California

Staying consistent and aligned with the fundamentals

So, we can see that there is a consistent theme across businesses that experience sustained growth and enduring success. They have a purpose, values and vision that remain fixed while their strategies, people, products and services adapt to the changing world around them. Maintaining these beliefs puts energy back into the business. It reinforces those beliefs. And it ensures they continue to inform their strategic decisions as a business going forward.

If you don't make this connection, you will see your business's energy dissipate. Staff will lose motivation as they start to question why they're working so hard. Customer loyalty will drop as they forget what your business stands for. Your partnerships will weaken, you will return to reactive strategies to get back on track, and the business will fall into a downward spiral.

As the leader we need to be very clear about the fundamentals (as we've laid out in each section of this book) that represent success for our business: holding up the beliefs, clarifying the strategic direction, committing to the priorities, installing the enablers, declaring the measures of success and holding the team to account. This requires consistent messaging, aligned actions and a cadence or rhythm that maintains the energy.

Telling stories

It's one thing to hold one-on-one meetings with our direct reports or gather our leadership team around a table, but how are you communicating across the wider business? Do you wheel out a spreadsheet full of figures or a hectic PowerPoint presentation oozing with facts, or do you tell great stories? There's currently a lot of buzz in businesses around storytelling through social media, though if you think about the countless generations and cultures that have passed down knowledge through stories over thousands of years it's rather strange that the business world is only now having a serious 'a-ha' moment about the value of storytelling in communication. Journalist Carolyn O'Hara has dissected the art of storytelling in the *Harvard Business Review*, suggesting that you first be clear on the audience you're targeting and the key 'one-line' message that you want them to walk away with. Then think about a mini-movie-script approach that brings in the emotions from real experiences, the struggles or conflicts along the way, and finish with an uplifting aspirational message. Remember to minimise the rational facts and figures, avoid too much detail, and allow time for practice (I recommend doing some practice with a video camera so you can get an audience perspective on how you present – watch for your speaking pace, body language, energy levels).

Remember, too, that there two sides to this. The story you are looking to tell about where the business is headed and what it must do to get there, and the stories that you need to collect ... about your team, a new product, a client success. A key part of leading at a business level is that increasingly the stories are about others. I remember how proud James Agius, the MD at Ecotech, was as he told me the story about the incredible teamwork at their Indian factory during COVID. In a short window of opportunity before the factory was locked down, they got a shipping container delivered, sourced beds, food and supplies so their staff could be safely isolated, who then worked long shifts to get the container filled with critical assemblies for client projects, and got it out the door in time. A story like this this will doubtless form part of the Ecotech legend. What are your stories?

In leading the business, the role becomes increasingly one of building the business brand, rather than the building the product/service brand that most likely got you started.

REMAINING TRUE TO YOUR CORE BELIEFS

Apple Computer Company was founded by Steve Jobs and Steve Wozniak in 1976. They built the original Apple I computer in Steve Jobs's parents' garage. This would later evolve into the Macintosh.

Released in 1984 for $2495, the Macintosh was the first affordable computer to offer a graphical user interface where icons and folders replaced text.

Through the eighties, Apple struggled as it faced competition from IBM and internal power struggles between Steve Jobs and then CEO John Sculley, which culminated in Jobs being stripped of all duties and forced out of Apple in 1985. Over the next twelve years the company would diversify into the Apple II and Macintosh product families, portable devices, printers and other accessories. However, with the rise of IBM and Microsoft's release of Windows 95, the company was in trouble.

In 1997, two months from bankruptcy, Jobs agreed to return to be the interim CEO. Within a year, Jobs cut the company back to a core suite of products and created an online store where customers could buy direct from the company. Then, once Apple had found stability as a niche provider, Jobs waited for 'the next big thing'. That ended up being online music, and in 2001 Apple released the first iPod and the iTunes store. From there the company launched a range of iPod products, including the iPod Touch, the Shuffle, the iPod Classic and the Nano.

This expansion built the financial base that Apple needed to launch its retail stores, its Safari web browser, the iPhone, the iPad and the Apple TV.

Most businesses are not like Apple. Most businesses struggle to grow beyond their initial products, industries and markets. While they may continue to grow within their market for some time, eventually they will hit maturity and begin the slow (or, in some cases, fast) decline into business death.

The difference between the Apples of the world and most businesses is that they have learned to *escalate*. They have learned to translate their existing success into new areas through a process of remaining true to their core beliefs, reflecting on what has worked to date, leveraging their strengths, and targeting the next big goal on the horizon.

They know their purpose. They know their values. They know their vision. And they know their competencies and how those map against gaps in the market.

As long as these elements remain, everything else a business does can change. It can branch into new industries, sell new products and services, hire new people and more. However, their beliefs remain constant and, in fact, propel them further.

Likewise, Apple's purpose is to challenge the status quo and think differently. Regardless of whether they're building a computer, a music player or a TV device, they uphold that purpose. And by upholding that purpose, the Apple customers who were so enamoured with earlier products will continue to line up outside their stores for six hours to buy new ones.

How will you shape the character, cadence and brand of your business?

KEY POINTS

1. The success of a business comes from aligning energy around what you believe, what you conceive and what you achieve as a group. This is enabled by clarifying the aspirations, ensuring activation and reinforcing through escalation.
2. The crucial central piece that governs performance, growth and value is leadership: how we lead ourselves, our team and at an organisational level.
3. Sadly, most business leaders lack insight on the key elements for success and the criticality of their own leadership in making it happen.
4. Our key role is to be clarifiers, simplifiers and enablers, telling a clear story about the image of success, being consistent and setting the cadence.
5. The greatest success is when it moves from being 'our' story as a leader and becomes 'theirs' as a team.

TAKE ACTION

Write down your thoughts about leading at a whole of business level.

1. How do you feel about your role as a leader of the business versus a 'technician' who happens to be in charge? What most needs to change in your own leadership as the business scales?
2. What parts of the business need your input to make them more collaborative and better aligned?
3. How must you develop the culture to support your organisational ambitions?

4. What is your biggest challenge communicating to the wider business? Is it public speaking, is it connecting across time zones and cultures, or perhaps it's tailoring a digestible message?
5. What does the brand of your business need in terms of leadership, distinct from what your products/services need?

Where to next?

My hope is that you'll take some insights from this book and make the changes that will grow your business to a new level. For some, that will be small tweaks while I imagine that others will want or need a more substantial overhaul to unlock the potential in front of them.

While it's still fresh, review the chapter summaries and reflective questions to discover key strengths you can leverage or gaps you can address. Where is the most significant opportunity for your business?

If there is no standout area for obvious and immediate action, my tip is to focus on the gaps in the Believe section first, then Conceive, and finally Achieve, as the energy you apply in each sphere is foundational for the next. Also, make sure that you tackle each of the 'propeller blades' in between, which will connect and enhance the actions in each area.

Growth is an important barometer of energy. While maintaining momentum is a challenge, there is a system to it. I've shared mine in this book. For further support and ideas, be sure to work through the Health Check companion to this book, available free at robertnankervis.com, and join the community of leaders who regularly receive my *Rob's Insights* column. For those who'd like more direct support, I offer speaking engagements, public workshops and in-house programs, the details of which are on my website.

One of my great privileges as a coach is watching my clients carefully working through the approach: getting clear on the beliefs they share, drawing out the essence of who they (and their clients) really are, crafting a model and strategy to bring out their best, setting themselves up to effectively deliver, valuing the lessons and celebrating the successes along the way as they grow their business and their own leadership towards its highest potential.

I wish you the same success as you propel the performance of your business.

Acknowledgements

When you spend most of your time at the strategic end of growth businesses, the detailed work of writing a book is a challenging exercise, especially as a first-time author.

I was fortunate, therefore, to have a support team to help me navigate the journey.

Daniel Priestley and Glen Carlson at Dent who, through their Key Person of Influence program, introduced me to an architecture for developing my business and personal brand, which included publishing a book.

Andrew Griffiths, my publishing and speaking coach, who laid out the roadmap for becoming an author, has been so generous in sharing his wisdom and experience, and kept me accountable for getting it done. There was a book in me after all AG!

Testing drafts is critical when so much of the writing process is introspective. In that regard, I am grateful to Geoff Green, Geoff Hetherington, Charles Martin and Rob Willis, who each provided valuable and discerning insights around my early ideas.

In a long process where it is hard to maintain momentum, it was handy to have an active Accountability Group. Geoff Green, Suzy Lee and Warren Otter were always there to test ideas, prod me with difficult questions (such as 'when is this book being published?') and encourage the next steps to get the final product done.

Jacqui Pretty had the wonderful editorial skills to take my performance model, ideas and lumps of text to build out the initial draft of the book and craft its structure. She also kept me accountable for actually getting the first manuscript done!

Adrian Potts then guided the manuscript skilfully through a significant edit, making a multitude of valuable recommendations to help me achieve a manuscript ready for final review.

Michael Hanrahan, Anna Clemann and the Publish Central team's editorial and publishing expertise pushed through the final edit and drew together the cover design, layout and printing to bring the manuscript to life as a published book.

My Content Manager Anne George used the book draft to develop ideas for many of the posts that we've put out on social media, and subsequently jumped in to help finish the case studies. Caroline Buffinton and the team at Aurora Creative have professionalised my branding and web presence, supported by the fine work of Beth Jennings' photography and Markus Ruefenacht's videos.

I'm grateful for the many friends I've made through the remarkable Key Person of Influence, Scaling Up, Coraggio and NextTech communities. To be able to exchange ideas with such clever and generous groups of colleagues is indeed a gift. I'm especially thankful to Verne Harnish, who has spent decades fostering the capability of mid-tier businesses around the world and created a platform for many of us as coaches to continue that service.

To the many colleagues and clients with whom I've worked and shared ideas over the last thirty-five years – I have learned much about business through these interactions, and our professional friendships have been a highlight of my career. In particular I'd like to recognise those client leaders who've engaged with my practice over multiple years: James Agius, Nick Beckett, Erik Birzulis, Daniel Crawford, Gaethan Cutri, Nicholas Dal Sasso, Stephen Ellich, Ross Gallagher, Damien James and Martin Stack. Thank you all for your valued support.

To the vast number of thought leaders I've met, whose seminars I've attended and whose works I've read, I am privileged in the work that I do to stand on the shoulders of these giants, and grateful for the wisdom that has been shared.

In closing, I want to acknowledge my family. My dad, Peter, was the first leader I knew and a wonderful benchmark for empathic leadership. My mum, Priscilla, was my coach before I knew how coaching worked, offering that essential mix of challenge and support. As parents, they instilled the values (especially persistence!), love and support that provided the foundation for everything else. To my siblings, Stephen and Sarah, I'm grateful for your ongoing support and encouragement, shared through an appropriate mix of nudges and niggles! Few are blessed with the extended family that I am privileged to enjoy and I am thankful to you all.

Thanks to my wife, Carmela, who has supported me throughout my professional career and its many demands, including the substantial time commitment in starting my own business and writing this book. I'm also grateful to my son, James, for the youthful energy and entrepreneurial inspiration he brings. The world needs more of his curious, creative, empathic leadership as the next generation takes the reins.

Finally, thanks to you, the reader, for being a leader who's a learner, seeking to amplify your impact and take your team and your business on the ride. I trust that the insights I've shared help you in your noble quest.

About Robert Nankervis

A business consultant, adviser, speaker and executive coach with thirty-five years' experience, Rob Nankervis specialises in guiding founder/owners, CEOs and senior executive teams in driving growth, overcoming performance challenges, and building value in their mid-size organisations.

In a career that has encompassed both senior functional leadership roles and a broad spectrum of consulting assignments, Rob has built the commercial acumen and communication skills to relate across industries and from shop floor to boardroom table.

Rob facilitates executive strategy retreats, leads quarterly team review sessions, coaches senior leaders, runs regular public training events and is sought as a speaker on leadership, performance and growth.

Before starting his own mid-tier advisory and coaching business in 2013, he was a Director of Performance Improvement within Ernst & Young's advisory practice and, prior to that, Client Partner and part-owner at boutique leadership advisory firm Oppeus International.

With qualifications in accounting and business, Rob is a Fellow of CPA Australia, the Institute of Company Directors, and the Governance Institute. He is a Certified International Coach with Scaling Up, a Certified Executive Coach, host of the Propelling Performance Podcast, and writer of the popular *Rob's Insights* leadership column. He has been appointed to the Global Advisory Board of Scaling Up.

Rob is driven by his purpose of helping other leaders achieve their highest potential, and making their organisations great places to work through illuminating possibility and facilitating change. His own BHAG is to positively impact 5000 businesses in the next fifteen years.

FREE RESOURCES

Access the free downloadable resources here:

robertnankervis.com/book

Use the code 'Propel'.

Join the community of leaders who are regular readers of my free *Rob's Insights* leadership column. It's a short and punchy handful of ideas that I send out twice each month to give you an edge.

Subscribe to my free 'Propelling Performance Podcast' where I share great content and ideas through interesting guest interviews.

COACHING

Rob offers his retained coaching program to a small number of new clients each year. If you'd like your business to be considered for this program, please contact Rob at the email address below.

Rob also offers standalone one- to three-day programs for leadership teams to help them break through their performance and growth challenges.

To enquire about these, contact coaching@robertnankervis.com.au.

EVENTS

Rob runs public events and masterclasses. Details are of upcoming events are here: robertnankervis.com/events.

SPEAKING

To have Rob speak with your organisation about the principles in Propelling Performance, email speaking@robertnankervis.com.au.

BULK ORDERS

For bulk orders of this book, email us at propelling@robertnankervis.com.au.

MORE FROM ROB

For more information about Rob, visit robertnankervis.com

You can also connect with Rob and follow the leadership insights he shares on the main social platforms:

linkedin.com/in/robert-nankervis
facebook.com/propellingperformance
@RobertNankervis

www.ingramcontent.com/pod-product-compliance
Lightning Source LLC
Chambersburg PA
CBHW071335210326
41597CB00015B/1462
9781922391216